HOW TO WRITE AND PUBLISH Your Own eBook... in as little as 7 Days!

"How to write and publish your own OUTRAGEOUSLY Profitable eBook in as little 7 days – even if you can't write, can't type and failed high school English class!"

JIM EDWARDS & JOE VITALE

NEW YORK

How to Write and Publish Your Own eBook in as Little as 7 Days

ISBN: 1-60037-152-3 (Paperback)
ISBN: 1-60037-189-2 (Hardcover)
ISBN: 1-60037-190-6 (e-Book)

Published by:

MORGAN · JAMES
THE ENTREPRENEURIAL PUBLISHER™

Morgan James Publishing, LLC
1225 Franklin Ave Ste 325
Garden City, NY 11530-1693
Toll Free 800-485-4943
www.MorganJamesPublishing.com

Cover and Interior Design by:
Tony Laidig
www.thecoverexpert.com
tony@thecoverexpert.com

LIMITS OF LIABILITY / DISCLAIMER OF WARRANTY:

Table of Contents

About the Authors

Jim Edwards

Jim Edwards is a dynamic and entertaining speaker who has developed, marketed and operated outrageously profitable online businesses for both himself and his clients worldwide since 1997.

Jim publishes a FREE no-holds-barred, "tell it like it is" multi-media newsletter at www.IGottaTellYou.com!

Jim is a frequent guest speaker nationally at conferences and seminars on such subjects as search engine and directory traffic generation, "shoestring online marketing" and more.

He is the author and co-creator of numerous highly successful ebooks and "info-products," including:

- **"5 Steps to Getting Anything You Want!"** Discover *The* 5-Step Goal Achievement System That Gives You A Positively Unfair Advantage In Business... and in Life!
- **"Turn Words Into Traffic"** How to write and publish articles online that bring an "avalanche" of website visitors and customers!
- **"eBook Secrets Exposed"** How to make massive amounts of money with your own ebook... whether you wrote it or not!

- **The Lazy Man's Guide to Online Business** How to Work Less... get Paid More... and have tons more Fun! Learn the Super "Lazy Achiever" Mindset!
- **How to Write and Publish your own eBook... in as little as 7 Days** "... even if you can't write, can't type and failed high school English class!"
- **Affiliate Link Cloaker Software** Keeps Internet "Pickpockets" from stealing your affiliate commissions!
- **Selling Your Home Alone** Sell your house yourself and save THOUSANDS in Realtor commissions!
- **The TEN Dirty Little Secrets of Mortgage Financing** How to save THOUSANDS in fees and unnecessary interest on your next mortgage loan!

Jim lives in Williamsburg, Virginia with his wife, daughter and five dogs.

He enjoys writing, walking, softball, playing video games and listening to Elvis, Frank Sinatra, and Willie Nelson.

Joe Vitale

Joe "Mr Fire" Vitale is an explosive "results only!" marketing consultant.

He has helped over 200 authors and publishers write, publish and promote their books.

He has also helped large companies, from The American Red Cross to Hermann Children's Hospital in Houston.

His reputation for writing powerful copy is well known:

- One of his sales letters achieved a record-breaking 91% response.
- One of his ads brought in 500 responses in only 30 days.
- A press release he wrote got a reporter to call only 7 minutes after it was released.

How does he do it?

See the secrets of success revealed in a series of helpful articles, right here, at **The Copywriting Profit Center**

Joe has written too many books to list here, including the brand new "Spiritual Marketing"—which people are calling a masterpiece—and "The Seven Lost Secrets of Success"—of which one company bought 19,500 copies!

Both books (along with many others) are available at **www.Amazon.com**

In addition, Joe is the author of the best-selling Nightingale-Conant audiotape program, **"The Power of Outrageous Marketing!"**

For more information about booking "Mister Fire!" as a speaker, or for more information, contact The Joe Vitale Agency in any of the following ways:

Email: joe@mrfire.com
World Wide Web: http://www.mrfire.com
Telephone: +1 (512) 847-3414
Fax: +1 281-999-1313

Mail: The Vitale Estate
121 Canyon Gap Rd.
Wimberley, TX 78676-6314

Let's Define an eBook

The term "ebook" gets thrown around pretty loosely on the Internet. At one end an ebook may contain only a one-page HTML document that someone threw together using a free compiler to turn into an "ebook". These ebooks rarely get into any serious level of detail and usually just entice the reader to go to a website and make a purchase –nothing more than a glorified sales letter.

We see nothing wrong with this type of ebook – however, we'll teach you how to write a much better product in as little as seven days.

The type of ebook we teach you how write in as little as seven days conveys complete information about a topic from start to finish. Your ebook will make the people who purchase it (or receive it as a bonus or giveaway on another purchase) feel as though they received a high level of value out of your publication.

Creating a ***high quality*** ebook will do two things for you:

1. It will put some serious money into your pocket with virtually no overhead... and...

2. Cut down on people asking for their money back! A high quality ebook gets far fewer returns than a low quality publication.

You are not going to learn how to write what my wife would term a "cheapo ebook"!

You will become a legitimate e-publishing author who gets paid for your work by following the information and the steps laid out in this course – and you will write and publish your book in 7 days or less!

You should understand that an excellent ebook – or even one just pretty good – can significantly and positively impact your life.

Nowadays everyday people, without any writing or publishing or type-setting skills, can create publications of value for which other people will willingly and eagerly pay money.

You can use the techniques in this book to create any type of ebook –

- Fiction
- Nonfiction
- History
- Mystery or more....

Our primary assumption in this course; that you want to create a book to sell through the web and will probably deal with some sort of "how to" type format... since this type of book sells most easily whether on-line or off line.

"How-to" books offer your best bet for a first time ebook or an ebook to up-sell to current and future customers, because these books solve a problem for the reader and gets rid of it for them.

We'll get into more detail on why "how to" books rate best a little later.

Why write an ebook?

Three good reasons why anybody writes any book.

First – To make profits! (The main emphasis of *this* ebook!)

We want to teach you how to do 3 things well:

1. Conceive an idea for an ebook that has a market with people willing to pay for it – either directly or indirectly;
2. Write your ebook quickly and concisely – and in a manner that conveys the information in a way people can use and implement quickly;
3. Take concrete action steps towards selling your book online by giving you a road map to start marketing your ebook on the Internet.

Second – To impress your customers or for prestige among your peers.

Prestige is a great thing… but it doesn't directly put money into your pocket – something that you really want to do!

Often, writing a book can be a significant credibility builder for you, however, while you get your e-publishing career off the ground, this probably shouldn't be the primary objective in writing your first ebook.

We advise you to write a best seller and make piles of cash. Then worry about writing the great American novel so you can brag to your friends.

Third – To use as a lead-in to another sale or as a follow-up sale to your existing customers.

This ties closely with the first reason for writing ebooks – making money!

Many successful e-publishers and authors keep a list of customers and past buyers and now focus their entire business on just creating new and valuable e publications for this existing list.

Every time they come out with a new publication they just announce the new ebook or info-product to their customer base and the sales start rolling in.

With a good publication (and no smart e-author releases anything but a good publication) they increase their credibility with their customers and, in the process, also make significant sales and generate revenue!

What results could you expect with a successful ebook?

As always, "success" is a relative term. Your version of success will vary greatly from my version of success – which will also vary greatly from your friends and business associates.

But let us tell you about some of Jim's success with writing an ebook...

I launched my first ebook, "Selling Your Home Alone", in the Fall of 1997.

"Selling Your Home Alone" teaches home sellers how to sell their own home without a real estate agent. I sell it at my **FSBO Help** website. (**www.fsbohelp.com**).

I wrote this ebook out of the expertise I gained in ten years as a mortgage broker and real estate agent. I was unaware of the techniques that we are going to teach you in this course and so writing that book took almost a year, because I wrote it when I had time and when the mood struck me.

The actual work time that went into writing the ebook took less than a week. I held myself back dramatically by the amount of editing that I wanted to do while writing the book... a problem we'll teach you how to overcome almost immediately.

To make a long story short, I made every mistake in the world in writing, publishing, and marketing that ebook online – yet despite these mistakes I made money... eventually awesome amounts of money!

Now after ironing out a system (a system we'll now lay out for you) I consistently make enough money from just that one ebook – which sells better than ever four years later – to cover our house payment, a car payment, and the electric bill... though I'm no longer actively working in the mortgage and real estate business at all!

Think, just ONE ebook!

I use past expertise and experience to make money and continue to make money well into the future! Now if that doesn't get you excited nothing will!

Now does that rate as a successful ebook?

I think so!

It gets better…

I wrote another ebook that follows up on that one called, "The TEN Dirty Little Secrets of Mortgage Financing," which I sell at **Mortgage Loan Tips (www.mortgageloantips.com)** – at least 20% of the people who buy my FSBO book end up purchasing this book as well, because once they sell their house they have to buy another… and 9 out of 10 buyers will need a mortgage!

My marketing costs to sell the mortgage book to my real estate customers—absolutely zero!

On another ebook / info-product project that I recently completed, we generated over $100,000 in gross sales in a little over 5 months. Though this slightly more complicated ebook involved videos, slide show presentations and multi-media – it took only two days to write!

Even after affiliate commissions and some minor product delivery costs (we deliver the information on CD) that product has a 60% net on gross sales – you do the math!

$60,000 clear profit in only about 5 months.

This continues as a very worthwhile project that makes money month after month with minimal effort now with the marketing systems in place!

Joe Vitale has experienced similar success with several of his publications....

"Can you really make any money with e-books?"

Until Stephen King put his short story online, available only as an e-book, the answer might be "No way."

Until then, people considered e-books as freebies. They were used mainly (and still are) to give people a reason to visit your website.

Advertise a free e-book at your website and people might go to your site to get it. That was, *and still is,* a valid marketing technique.

But make any money from an e-book? Not likely… until recently!

Stephen King woke up the online world and shook the publishing industry. Within 24 hours of announcing his online short story, which sold for $2.50, more than 400,000 people bought it! King made more than a million dollars within three days.

This impressed even King, who couldn't download his own e-book because he uses a Mac and not a PC.

But many authors make money with e-books.

Sales for my own "Hypnotic Writing" e-books (**Hypnotic Writing: www.hypnoticwriting.com** and **Advanced Hypnotic Writing: www.advanced-hypnoticwriting.com**) continue to amaze and delight me.

When the text first went online, I truly didn't expect a single order for the $29.95 product. But within an hour, nearly 100 people ordered it!

And within a day or so, more than 600 people invested their money for it. And as of this writing, about three months later, my e-book produced more than $45,000— and the orders keep coming!

No wonder I smile most of the time these days.

Yet King and I aren't the only people to cash in on the Internet's latest and hottest trend.

Look at how well Jim Edwards does with his books and information products online.

My friend David Garfinkel, a copywriter and marketing consultant, put his course on how to write copy online – **Killer Copy Tactics (www.killercopytactics.com)**.

Within two months he made $35,000 in sheer profit. (Note that I said: **SHEER PROFIT**)

Keep in mind that all of this profit is *passive* income.

King, Garfinkel, Jim and myself don't print books, fulfill orders, warehouse products, or anything else. We wrote our books once and now continuously sell what we wrote.

Money comes to us no matter what we do… my idea of prosperity!

Okay. So e-books offer a valid way to make money — at least for people like King, Garfinkel, Jim Edwards and myself.

But what about you?

Can YOU make money with your own e-book?

Obviously, I believe the answer to be yes, so we wrote this book. We want to help you write, distribute, promote and sell your own money-making e-book.

Read these lessons, do what we ask of you, and you too can join the ranks of e-authors making a nice income with e-books.

One last thing before we get started… Motivation!

Anthony Robbins, the famous success coach, talks a lot about the power of "why"!

"Why" you do something, far outweighs the "how," you will get it done.

When your brain picks out a target with a strong enough "why" to go for it – you will achieve your goal. You will find the help, you'll get the education, you'll seek out the experts and do whatever it takes to make it over the top.

We don't think you would purchase this book unless you wanted to make a change in your life for the better. You wouldn't invest in a book and even read this far unless you believed you could get the results you wanted – specifically your own ebook which you wrote and can sell for money on the Internet.

The biggest problem anyone overcomes: procrastination in getting started on the project.

Overcome that procrastination with a big enough "why"!

If you can't get motivated enough to overcome your procrastination on writing your ebook just by thinking about the rewards you'll get in terms of money you could or want to make, try a different approach.

Picture an actual result you want to achieve and make that picture big and bright and hold it right in front of you.

Close your eyes right now and visualize what a successful ebook would mean to you.

What do you see?

Think about what writing and successfully marketing your ebook and setting up a "remote control" business, will bring you in terms of other rewards, such as:

- Prestige
- Respect
- A new car
- An exotic vacation
- Freedom

We want you to set what you would consider realistic goals up front. Then we also want you to constantly strive to improve your results, increase your sales and develop new products for your customer list using the techniques that we'll outline for you in this book.

Also, one book can't answer every single question you could ever have about a certain subject. We want to teach you the techniques we (and many others) use regularly to write excellent ebooks in a VERY short time and publish them for the web.

In doing this we will leave no stone unturned and you will understand exactly what to do and how to do it to get your ebook written and ready for sale.

We also provide some of the most effective marketing tips and techniques you can use to market and sell your ebooks – but please understand one thing – entire books already exist about *each* of the techniques we will outline.

The most powerful suggestion we can make after finishing your ebook: embark upon a course of study that will constantly lead you to new and innovative ebook marketing techniques, tools and resources that will surely come along in the very near future.

Let's get started!

Setting Yourself up for Success

The single biggest most catastrophic mistake we see the authors making once they decide to write an ebook for profit is deciding on a topic for their ebook without giving any thought – let alone research – to the actual market.

If nobody will buy the ebook or even show some interest – DON'T write it!

We know people who spent mountains of money, energy and effort in creating publications with no one else interested in reading them!

They use this formula to create their ebooks.

eBook Failure Formula

1. Write a book
2. Look for a market
3. **Pray**
4. Get mad and give up!

Now, if you are already independently wealthy and have plenty of money this is a fine formula – but if you want to *make* money then you

need to take a hard look at the market and create your ebook in a way that meets the *needs* of that market.

By the way, this problem has plagued authors since time began!

Somebody gets a "great idea" for the next best novel ever – only to find it doesn't interest anyone, with no way they could get published and nobody buys the book.

There's nothing wrong with writing on a subject that interests you – just don't expect everyone else to be interested unless you do your homework first!

The formula for creating a "successful" ebook?

eBook Success Formula

1. Identify a niche market
2. Analyze their wants, needs and problems
3. Write the book that satisfies their wants by meeting their needs and solving their problems
4. Market the book directly to your niche market and make MONEY!

Let's take a look at each part of the formula…

Step 1 – Identify a Niche Market (people who need you!)

A "niche market" includes a highly defined group of people you can easily identify online.

They visit the same sites, they read the same ezines, they post to the same forums, they use the same download sites, etc.

A niche market represents your best chance for success because you can find the people to sell your ebook to without spending a million dollar TV advertising budget!

If you try to please all people you will fail miserably. You're too small to be Wal-Mart… that's why all the dot-com's failed. They tried to service *all* people's needs and ended up actually needed by very *few* people!

So do your homework and identify a group of people with a common interest or problem.

Common interests can include anything:

- Cooking
- Real Estate
- Dog breeds
- Online Marketing (over-done at this point)
- Model plane building
- Genealogy – Family Trees
- Past military service
- Small, pre-teen, teenage children
- Investing
- Music
- Exercise, health, lifestyle
- Online auctions

Problems can include:

- How to accept credit cards in your online store even on a shoestring budget.
- How to find the right breed of dog.
- How to come up at the top of the search engines.

- How to care for plants / the best type of plants for busy people.
- How to get traffic to your website.
- How to research your family tree online.
- How to research effectively in a given area of interest
- Where to find replacement parts for old cars
- Where to find alternative treatments for a child with ADD

The number of possible niche markets to pick from are positively endless – but you must identify them first.

1. Pick one which *really* interests you and ask yourself a few questions:
2. What is the real size of the market? How big is it?
3. Will the size of the group warrant writing an ebook?
4. Will the target audience willingly pay for the information / knowledge / instruction I will provide in my ebook?

If they won't pay very much for the information, can I "back-end" the book so it will bring revenue from sales I make as a result of their original book purchase?

Once you identify a suitable niche market then move on to Step 2 in the formula…

Step 2 – Analyze their wants, needs and problems

So how do you find out what the market wants?

Take the easiest way and ask them – just ask!

Jim Edwards analyzed the market ***and*** wrote his ebook "The TEN Dirty Little Secrets of Mortgage Financing" in a week just by first going around to about 45 real estate agents he knew and asking them to tell him the mortgage questions buyers most frequently asked them.

Jim called on those agents and instead of a boring sales call he actually engaged them in a fun process of asking and answering questions. He even told them about writing a book and for helping him out he would give them a free copy!

He then took those questions, organized them, and answered each of them with the same information he gave away for free over the phone and in person to potential borrowers, in the hope that someone would hire him to do their mortgage loan.

He took the *same* questions he answered over and over and simply wrote down the answers in an organized fashion.

> "Before I knew it the ebook was done and I've been selling it online and offline ever since!"

So how do you ask people what they want and the problems they need solved?

Since you will most likely sell your ebook online, start by using the Internet to help you discover the answers!

People gather online in many different places to exchange information and look for help, such as:

- Forums
- Chat rooms
- Ezine lists
- Bulletin boards
- News Groups and more!

In these areas you can learn what interests them. Also, keep your eyes peeled for survey results. That marketing data can prove worth its weight in gold for you in looking for problems people need solved.

For example: If 80% of targeted users surveyed express a similar preference, problem or interest, you may lock onto a winner! If only 10% of target-

ed users surveyed show an interest in something, you've got a dead duck and should keep looking!

Online, site owners can easily take surveys of their past customers or users of a certain service. You can find many of these survey results at their sites and use them as very valuable marketing intelligence.

The question probably running through your mind right this minute; "OK where do I find the survey results?"

You find them on the sites these people visit!

Will all of the sites keep surveys where you can see them? No! But a lot of sites do carry surveys on them and often you can see how people answered the survey if you take part.

If you already operate a site you might consider adding a brief survey to start gathering marketing and user opinion data.

If you can't find any survey results or don't operate a site of your own, consider approaching various site owners in your niche market and see if they want to do a survey.

You may find some future joint venture partners if you explain the value they could get from gathering this marketing data and use this initial contact to start building a relationship.

Compare your niche market to an animal you hunt through the forest. Members of that group leave a trail of clues because they go certain places, look at certain things, read particular ezines and other specific publications.

Example:

Let's look at a real Niche Market – "Online auction sellers"

- This group probably includes a large number of eBay users. These people go to certain sites such as eBay and Auction Watch.
- They may also use certain software tools such as Marketplace Manager.

- These users probably also congregate around the auctions at Amazon.com, Excite, MSN, Yahoo and others.
- They may subscribe to certain Usenet "news groups" such as: **alt.marketing.online.ebay**

  NOTE: You can search through thousands of newsgroups at http://groups.google.com/
- Just by going where they go... reading what they read... and seeing what they see, you can recognize ebook opportunities.

The best and fastest way to spot an opportunity; **look for a problem**!

Now what do I mean when I say, "Look for a problem."?

Critical Principle to Understand:
Problems represent opportunities in the world of ebook creation.

If you look in any successful ebook it likely solves a problem for a specific target market. So if you can find a problem for a large number of people and solve that problem quickly and effectively – you get your "winner" ebook!

So take a look at your target market.

Their needs?

What do they need to know how to do?

Their pains and real troubles?

What problem do they all encounter on a regular basis?

Step 3 – Write a book that satisfies their wants / solves their problems

The whole purpose and the main focus of this ebook will teach you how to write your own ebook that brings enormous value to the table for your readers.

Make sure your ebook focuses on your readers and write it with their needs in mind, including:

- Quickly solving their obvious problems;
- Solving "hidden" problems, once they see and understand them they will definitely want the solution;
- Using the words and language they use – not the complicated technical terms you use "in the business". Make sure you write in terms your audience uses in their everyday communication, so they won't struggle to understand you;
- Making sure your text communicates in a way that conveys your ideas quickly and in usable form;
- You provide a real value for the money they spend with you.

Step 4 – Market Directly to your Niche Market and make MONEY

The first step in marketing your ebook?

Figure out how and where your niche market will search for their information online.

What sites will they visit?

What keywords will they enter into the various search engines?

You must get very familiar with the types of keywords people will use when searching for information to solve their problem – the problem you will get paid for solving in your ebook!

These critical keywords will also allow people to find you when they do searches at online bookstores, search engines and download sites.

You will want to use the words they use, so you come up in their searches. Do some research at various online bookstores.

As examples you can check out, just click on each bookstore below and do some searches. See how each bookstore behaves when you search around.

Do they list alphabetically?

Do they use a "search engine" within the site?

How do they list their books and decide who comes up first when you look around?

- The eBook Mall
- Cyber Read
- Book Locker

Here's a link at Yahoo! you can check that has dozens and dozens and DOZENS of ebook stores covering all nature of topics!

http://dir.yahoo.com/Business_and_Economy/Shopping_and_Services/Books/Bookstores/Electronic_Books/

NOTE: After publication some of these links may go down because the Internet moves so fast! If one of these links goes down please send us an email and we'll check it out. If we end up making a change to the book we'll send you a new, updated copy free of charge!

Observe how various books show up in the searches and you'll notice in many cases the authors used – either by accident or on purpose – the keywords you input for the search in their title and description.

With the following links you can do actual keyword research online.

These tools allow you to see what people search for and the related words they use.

Pay attention to the special link on Overture (a pay-per-click search engine) where you can see actual counts of how many times someone searched for a phrase last month on Overture. This will really help you compare the relative popularity of various keyword phrases.

Click here ====> http://inventory.overture.com (www.Overture.com)

I cannot stress the importance of understanding which keywords your target niche looks for, so you can place yourself in front of people while they search for information.

For example:

Let's say you want to promote a free chapter of your book.

You must know your vital keywords when someone searches on a download site or a bookstore and starts typing in key words. What you named your file and the keywords you placed in your title and description will determine whether they can even find you or not.

Since many sites also factor in the popularity of your download (how many times people get your file) you must make yourself as easy to find as possible by using a "keyword rich" file name, title and description until your file becomes popular and gets that additional popularity boost.

Let's say for example you sell a book about how to sell your own home. The majority of your prospects might use the word "house" when searching and surfing the Internet, however all of *your* documentation uses the word "home".

Using the word "home" will decrease the likelihood that people can find you in the various places they'll be looking, because you don't use *their* words to communicate!

Successful ebook marketers understand that real and lasting success comes from talking the language of your prospects – not by forcing them to talk your language.

We've listed two very popular download sites you should take some time to explore and perform various searches. Pay attention to how the files show up, in what order, and the criteria these sites seem to use to determine which files come up first and why.

Click here ====> www.zdnet.com

Click here =====> www.downloads.com

How do the keywords you searched for relate to the results you got back from the site's search engine?

Don't just look at the file names and the one line descriptions, click on the individual results and look at the full descriptions for the files you find.

How many times do you see your keyword search words and related terms in the title and description of the files?

We'll talk a lot more about specific marketing techniques in a later chapter, but you must understand the words your customers will use when searching for your material on download sites and in online bookstores.

You may never offer a free chapter of your book as a marketing technique, but take a few minutes now and do a little research to get a feel for how things work. It will definitely help you in more ways than one.

One more point about marketing directly to your target niche market.

By using the words and specific terminology of your niche market, you more easily communicate your solutions to their problems in your sales letter. Because you use the words they use – and define their problems in terms they easily understand – it will make it much easier for you to make a sale.

So if you want to set yourself up to succeed with your ebook, make sure you:

1. Target your audience and identify a niche.
2. Define their problems based on what they tell you through their behavior, polls, forums and other online information sources. Do not define their problems based on what you "think, hope or guess" about their problems.
3. Learn the words they use to communicate so you speak their language.

4. Solve their problems and communicate your solutions effectively to them in your marketing.

Do all this and you will find a very high probability of success at writing, publishing and selling your ebook!

How to pick your topic

Though we cover picking your topic in the seven day writing method section – we want to address this very critical topic in some detail before you start to outline your book and going through the process of writing the text.

One of the fastest ways to get your ebook out of your head and into the computer so people can start paying money for it, uses an existing area of expertise or interest you already possess.

Maybe it's something you do well in your work; a hobby or some special skill. Often these skills and interests form the knowledge base necessary to write a book quickly and easily – probably more quickly and easily than you could ever imagine.

Let me ask you a few questions:

- What do you do best at work?
- What can you do better than 90 percent of all other people?
  - Maybe not better than everybody in the industry you work in or in a hobby, but if someone wanted to find out more about what you do or how you do it and had no knowledge in the area, they would automatically consider you an expert—no matter what level the word "expert" might mean?

- What can you get emotional about? Emotion is the single most POWERFUL force you can put into writing an ebook or any other publication!
  - What do you love?
  - What do you hate?

Often people can get more emotional about things they hate than things they love!

Positive or not, emotion causes people to create great novels as well as excellent how-to books.

Anything someone can get emotional about, will charge their writing with conviction! Even if people don't agree with you they will respect the fact that you feel strongly about the issue.

Something you feel very strongly about will cause you to do the necessary research and act emphatically about your explanation of the facts as you see them.

You will leave no stone unturned and will explain the various related issues and procedures in a complete and compelling way for your reader.

Very often a subject about which you can get extremely emotionally involved, works as the best subject for your first ebook.

Take a minute right now and just think about something that you feel very strongly about emotionally, that might serve as the topic of your first ebook, once we actually get into the seven day writing method.

What would you like to learn more about?

After you became an expert in that area would this topic make others pay you for sharing your newfound knowledge?

With so much information available online no one can know and find everything on their own – and there lies your opportunity!

Believe it! People will pay you for information they could find on their own. If paying you $29, $39 or $49 will save them time and give them the information they want quickly and in a form they can act on immediately, you've got a customer.

Find some issue – especially in the online world – you want to know more about; probably other people will want to know about it too.

NOTE: Just make sure before you pile in 100 hours worth of work on an ebook, you figure out how people will search for information and whether enough people will search to make it worthwhile to write about it.

Be careful of your time and make sure to gauge how much time and money you should invest in the project.

The best thing to do if you decide to create an ebook out of a research project?

First research the subject, take excellent notes and write your findings as if you intend to explain what you discovered to a friend.

Now in this case it will not look like the boring, snoring research papers you used to hand over in college and high-school!

Pretend this information will go to a friend whom you want sincerely to guide down the same path to get the great results or information you found.

- First define the problem you want to solve or the result you intend to accomplish.
- Next how did you find the solutions?
- Finally, how can the people reading your ebook use what you discovered to save time, make money, avoid effort and achieve better results in their life?

The best type of eBook to write

The best type topic or format for an ebook uses the "How To" approach.

The "how to" format works so well online because people go online to find information they can use – *FAST*!

During the Internet's recent past – say in 1996 to 1999 – most people who went online expected to get information absolutely free and many (not all) got offended when they came across the opportunity to pay for information.

However, recently the Internet jammed up with information so badly that researching any subject online can take hours if not weeks to find the information you want.

NOTE: If you don't believe this fact on overcrowded sites and information, go to the nearest search engine and type in the phrase "computer technical support" and see how many sites come up!

People finally realized that if someone can show them exactly how to accomplish what they want to get done online and provide it to them in an organized, logical ebook format – they'll pay to avoid hours and hours researching the subject.

If the subject of the ebook is on how to do something people will pay for that information even if they know they could do their own research and find the majority of the information online.

The convenience and "expert" help justifies the cost of buying a how to ebook as opposed to endlessly searching for the information online, especially when they need a quick solution!

Why People Buy eBooks

Let's take a look at the reasons people buy.

The following three pages list the top reasons people buy just about anything, especially information.

These reasons generally rate in this order of importance amongst direct marketers – the people who understand how to communicate in print in a way that makes people buy!

Number 1 – To Make Money

The number one reason people buy anything, especially online; they think it will help them make more money.

Why did you buy this ebook?

Probably you bought this ebook because you felt like it would help you create your own ebook that would in turn make *you* money – an excellent reason to buy an ebook!

Someone jokingly said not too long ago that the way to make a million dollars online was by writing a book about how to make a million dollars online and sell it. That actually comes quite close to the truth.

Fortunately people now realize that unless you can prove you know your stuff and can build credibility quickly with them, they won't take your information too seriously or buy your ebook.

Number 2 – To Save Money

The second most common reason for buying something; they think it will help them save money.

Jim's first ebook, "Selling Your Home Alone," covered only one topic – how to save the Real Estate Broker Commission that usually costs sellers anywhere from $4,500 to over $20,000.

Over a million people a year try to sell their house themselves before hiring an agent, so that niche market will probably never dry up.

Many ebooks succeed with topics about how to save money.

Number 3 – To Save Time

Everybody only gets 24 hours in a day. It sounds obvious, but it's true, now more than ever!

Many software automation programs sell so well online for this reason. They can automate tasks that people otherwise would devote hours and hours getting done. Show people how to save time and still get the same or better results they want and you get the basis for a solid ebook.

Number 4 – To Avoid Effort

Excluding lazy people, most individuals realize they just can't get

everything done in one day. If you can show them how to do things with the least amount of effort, you get a winner ebook.

Number 5 – To Get More Comfort

If people think your information will get them more of what they want, they may buy it.

Number 6 – To Achieve Greater Cleanliness / Hygiene

Why do you think people buy so much dishwashing detergent, laundry detergent, deodorant, perfume, shampoo, razors, shaving cream and foot powder?

Because they want to achieve a greater level of cleanliness in their lives!

Could you show someone how to live a better, cleaner life?

Number 7 – To Attain Fuller Health.

The huge number of diet books and diet programs available on and offline, forms a multi-billion dollar part of our economy... and that trend continues.

If you can write an ebook that helps someone in the area of health, weight management, beauty etc. then you may get your winner.

NOTE: This industry is pretty crowded so make sure you target your niche market carefully! Also, exercise extreme caution in making any medical or other claims you can't back up with proven scientific facts.

Number 8 – To Escape Physical Pain

Anyone with chronic pain or nagging physical problems you can remedy by information that you write, would likely purchase your ebook – if they believed they could get the result they wanted.

*NOTE: Think **very** carefully about making any types of medical claims in your ebooks that you can't substantiate or quote some sort of medical documentation to back you up. Carefully check the claims you make regarding any information you write in an ebook, and doubly so when dealing with health-related issues.*

Number 9 – To Gain Praise

If someone buys a new house or a new car, they usually brag to their friends and family, so their friends will praise them for making an excellent decision.

Often people want to brag about what a great deal they got or how they bargained the salesperson down a whole bunch.

If someone can buy your ebook and as a result get some sort of praise or recognition from people whose opinion they value, then you get a winner.

Number 10 – To be Popular

This one goes along with No. 9 to some degree. If you can show people how to gain popularity, whether at work, home or in a social setting, you may create an avalanche of new sales by filling that need.

Now each of these 10 reasons taken individually can create a compelling basis for people to purchase your ebook. However if you can combine one or more of these buying motivations into your ebook then you drastically increase your chances of creating an ebook that will appeal to a large audience and result in the greatest number of sales.

If you can show people how to make money, how to save money and how to save time while avoiding effort – you own something valuable!

If you can show people how to get more comfort, achieve fuller health and escape pain then you found the basis for a successful book!

Ask yourself this question right now, but don't feel bad if the answer doesn't pop right into your brain. Probably the first time you ask yourself this question your brain will say "I haven't got a clue." or "This doesn't

make any sense." but just keep asking the question and trusting that an answer will come to you in due time.

The question:

"What do I know how to do – or what would I like to know how to do – that would combine two or more of these reasons people buy, which I could then turn it into an exciting and valuable ebook?

Think about that for a while.

The answers you get will definitely excite you and get your mind percolating like a boiling coffee pot... some of our students report they have a little trouble sleeping once the great ideas start bubbling up out of their minds. It's a very exciting process!

Look at these examples of ebooks people wrote and marketed that illustrate meeting the needs of these 10 reasons to buy.

What ideas can they give you?

Title: Hunting For Mr. Good Bargain

Author: Marlene M. Moore
Here in this little book are the answers to your shopping questions: How can I find the best bargains? How can I dress within my budget? How can I find that perfect gift? How can I be a successful mail order shopper? How can I shop on the Internet?
Price: $10.95
Format(s): PDF (ebook) | Paperback
Pages: 132
http://www.booklocker.com/books/861.html

Title: The Virtual MBA

Author: C.J.Kasis
A comprehensive coverage of the skills needed by today's business managers, from E-commerce to Accounting to Supply Chain Management
Price: $14.50

Format: pdf
Pages: 102
http://www.booklocker.com/bookpages/cjkasis01.html

Title: **WorkInsight: A Headhunter's Guide to Finding the Perfect Job**
Author: David Perry
Leads you through a simple, guided process for picking your most productive skills for your next employer AND for your own future.
Ebook Price: $19.95
Format: PDF
Pages: 151
http://www.booklocker.com/books/958.html

Title: **Wake 'em Up: How to Use Humor and Other Professional Techniques to Create Alarmingly Good Business Presentations**
Author: Tom Antion
Are you one of the millions of people who dread creating business presentations? And after you've presented, do you feel you just didn't command the attention you needed to get your points across? Finally, help is here.
Price: $19.95
Format: pdf
Pages: 301
http://www.antion.com/wakebook.htm

Title: **How to Find More Ancestors Through Online Networking**
Author: Nancy Hendrickson
You'll find everything you want to know about becoming an expert Internet genealogical networker. Learn how to find the other researchers who are looking for you! Network with distant cousins, find new family lines. Written in easy-to-follow steps.
Price: $8.95
Format: pdf
http://www.booklocker.com/bookpages/nhendrickson.html

Title: LAID OFF? Find a Job and Find it Fast!

Author: Robert Daugherty

The title says it all…. Find a job fast if you've been laid off from your last one!

Price: $8.95

Format: PDF

Pages: 88

http://www.booklocker.com/books/631.html

Title: How to Find Your Own Pot of Gold Trading Stock Options

Author: M. C. Franklin

Is there a conservative stock trading strategy that wins 80% of the time? Is it possible to buy stocks at discount or double the income on stocks you already own? Yes, with options.

Price: $12.95

Format: pdf

Pages: 70

http://www.booklocker.com/books/1391.html

Title: How to Save Money When Building or Buying a Home

Author: Abbisoft Multimedia, Inc.

This guide shows you how to save money when building or buying a home and how to get the best prices on labor and materials.

Price: $9.95

Format(s): PDF (ebook)

Pages: 103

http://www.booklocker.com/books/510.html

Title: How To Have Great Sex While Cleaning Your House, and 23 other fun and profitable how-to ideas for creative (and desperate) people

Author: Lisa Tyler

A humorous look at real ways to make money, improve your life and have better sex, all on a working girl's salary... Contains 24 amazing chapters.

Price: $12.95
Format: PDF
Pages: 63
http://www.booklocker.com/books/1297.html

We will cover the mechanics of how to quickly write your ebook in the chapter on "The 7 Day eBook Writing Method". There we guide you step-by-step through the seven day process of conceiving the book, organizing your ideas, writing the ebook, editing and finally publishing the book for online distribution.

But for now – just enjoy the ideas that come to you and write down the ones that seem the most appealing!

The 7 Day eBook Writing Method

Get Ready to Rock!

Fact! The title of "author" can help skyrocket you into the big leagues! A book gives you real credibility that adds to the bottom line in prestige and money for yourself and your business!

It doesn't matter if you self-publish your book, pay your own printing bill or create an ebook you publish on the web. Clients only care that you look like the expert because you literally "wrote the book on it."

No one can deny that anyone who writes a book rates as an authority on the subject of that book. Our society respects and reveres authors; for hundreds of years in fact!

By following this simple process for writing your ebook and by following the rest of the advice in this course, you will produce your own book-length electronic publication on a subject and in a form people will want to purchase online!

Before we get started let's take a look the three most common objections or doubts you might feel about your ability to write anything remotely resembling a book!

Objection Number 1 – "You can't write"

You don't need to know how to write – at least not in the traditional sense – and certainly not in the world of rules and grades you remember from high school and college!

You just need to know how to explain things to people in a conversational tone. Relax! "Writing" means explaining things to people in a way that makes them feel comfortable and allows them to understand and use your information.

Stop worrying about your writing ability and pretend you want to explain something to a close friend over a cup of coffee or a beer.

You can write well – we promise!

Objection Number 2 – "You don't have anything to say"

Why do people do business with you?

They do business with you because you can answer their needs!

They come to you for answers to their questions about plumbing, real estate, painting, insurance, banking or whatever you happen to do – people need these questions answered.

Take the answers to those questions and use them as the basis for a book.

- As an accountant you might write a book on five ways to save money on your taxes.
- A chiropractor might write a book on 10 ways to prevent back injury.
- The owner of a restaurant might write a book revealing some of the secrets in his or her more popular recipes.

Something – we guarantee it – in your business life or hobbies can turn into a book that a specific group of people would eagerly pay money for a copy.

Keep in mind that you are NOT giving away the farm here. You give away and actually get paid for providing sound practical advice, that in the process promotes you and your business as the experts.

This will help you no matter if you own an offline business or if you strictly publish for the Web.

Becoming known as "the expert" opens up a "back end" for you to make sales of additional products for years to come. You can either develop these products yourself or you can find other people's products that interest your audience and offer them to your people for a share of the profit.

Either way you win as the expert in the eyes of the people who buy and read your ebook.

Objection Number 3 – "You don't want to write a full-length book"

No problem! You can stop well short of creating *War and Peace*.

Joe's best selling book ever, *Turbo Charge Your Writing*, runs only 22 pages long! Incredibly, two of those pages are order forms for ordering more copies of the book. The actual text for that book can fit on the front and back of two single spaced typewritten pages, but the content is so powerful that that book just went into its eighth printing!

You can write a short and sweet ebook too – just make sure that people get their money's worth!

We know a person who published an ebook only seven pages long, yet he consistently sells it for between $30 and $50 with very few returns.

He succeeded with this ebook because he wrote on a subject that almost every single person who wants to do business on the Internet must address at some point in their business life – the high cost of setting up merchant accounts and accepting credit cards.

This gentleman's book outlines various sources and companies that enable online publishers of information and software – as well as those selling physical products – to accept credit cards without the huge up-front fees that range from between $200 and $500 just to get started.

To make matters worse, these merchant accounts then obligate you to sign a contract where you pay between $30 to $50 a month for 4 to 5 years – whether you ever sell anything or not! Saving this high cost helped this man launch a highly successful ebook.

He started out looking for information he thought was readily available but he couldn't find it anywhere. Once he put in all the effort to find what he needed, he then compiled what he found.

He started selling his "research project" to people who would rather pay for his research instead of investing the weeks and weeks of frustrating research time it took to find all these various ways of accepting credit cards with no up-front fees and no minimum monthly fees.

You don't need a long book with your name on it – you want an ebook with extremely valuable content that people want to buy!

So how do you write an ebook?

Much easier than you think!

Follow this plan of action – making adjustments as you feel you need to – and you will finish a complete draft of a new ebook in only a matter of days!

Ready?

Let's get started!

Day 1 – In the beginning

First Things First!

Pull out a sheet of paper and make a list of everything that you might ever want to write a book about.

Jot down any ideas – no matter how silly they may seem right now.

Keep in mind that this is for your eyes only. Nobody will grade your topics. Feel free to write down any crazy idea, point or thought.

You want to create a list of anything you might possibly ever, in your wildest dreams write a book about. Anything goes!

Enjoy yourself – but make sure that you write down anything and everything that you could ever possibly write a book about. You'll find when you finish with your first ebook and achieve some success – you'll want to write another!

So find out now – from the deepest reaches of your subconscious mind – all the things that you might ever want write a book about, because this list will make your fortune and bring you more happiness and fulfillment than you could ever imagine at this point.

Even if you already know what you want to write a book about – still do this exercise!

This will help you to clarify things in your own mind and will probably bring out some additional ideas for the book you didn't consider before now.

Once you finish the list and you feel your mind has given its all, take a break, relax for a few minutes and then move on to the next step.

Now look over your list.

What ideas seem more attractive to you than others?

What would you consider writing a book about now, even if you didn't have everything "together" before you began? Which idea excites you the most?

Circle the titles and the ideas that seem most magnetic and exciting to you. Again, just let go and enjoy!

Now scan your list of circled titles. If you circled more than one idea – no problem! Can you combine the circled ideas into one book idea?

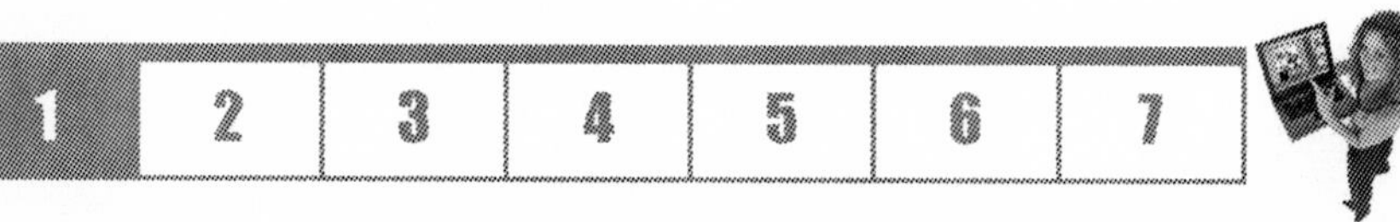

If not, or if it doesn't feel right, does one idea seem more appealing to you than another?

At this point try to pick just one idea that you would ***really*** like to write about. I suggest you trust your intuition on this one. Your mind may suggest you write about something because it makes sense, but your heart may point to another idea because your real interests lie there. Go with your heart! You'll write a better book and enjoy doing it if you listen to your heart.

Decision Time!

Now lose all the doubt in your mind and choose one idea. If you can't pick one then just put them in a hat and then pick one. Once you choose let go of all the doubt and get excited! You are about to create something wonderful and magical that will go way beyond you and your life right now.

NOTE: Don't trash the list of book ideas you don't use right now. Carefully put it somewhere you can find later. You will probably come back to it and write another book sometime in the near future – especially if it relates to the topic of the first book you want to write now.

A Focus Statement – The Critical Step

Now let's create a focusing statement to guide your thinking and enlist the power of your subconscious mind for the book you're about to write.

Here you decide ***exactly*** on your intention for creating your ebook.

Do you want to write a 100 page, how-to book, for salespeople to boost your career or teach them new skills?

Do you want to write a 75 page book teaching people little known facts about your industry or profession that will save them time or make them money?

Do you want to write a book that profiles successful people in your industry and gets them to reveal their tips, tricks and methods for success?

Do you want to write a 50 page inspiring teaching tale that will instruct people on a certain subject such as:

- Cooking
- Painting
- Insurance / financial planning
- E-publishing
- Accepting credit cards online
- Operating an online business effectively
- How to trace your genealogy using tools available online
- Home improvement
- Any other niche market subject!

I also want you to create an intention or definite outcome for yourself as a result of writing the book.

What do you *really* want from your ebook?

- Do you want to make a hundred thousand dollars?
- Do you want the book to help you achieve a greater degree of financial independence while helping others?
- Do you want the book to change lives?
- Do you want the book to impress your peers?

Create a focusing statement as an affirmation of your goal for your ebook project.

This statement will explain exactly what you want to achieve with your book, whom you want to impact and what you want to happen for you as a result.

Look at the actual focusing statement we used for this book:

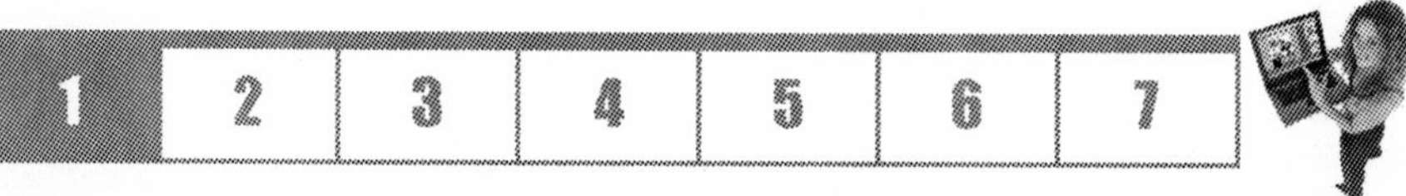

"To create a comprehensive, easy-to-understand and useful tool that guides anyone to conceptualizing, writing, publishing and marketing their own ebook in as little as 7 days – even if they can't write, can't type and have only a couple of hours a day to devote to the task."

Don't skip this VERY important part of the process!

Take a few moments to iron out a statement that feels right to you, but don't let this stop you either.

If you can't state your goal in a totally comfortable way, do the best you can and then let it go for now.

Congratulations!

You actually completed the most important step in the entire 7 Day eBook Writing Method!

Now, with a focusing statement, your subconscious mind will work on your project while you go about your day, take a shower, take a nap – whatever!

The power of your subconscious mind can now, like a homing missile, go about its mission of hitting the target you just placed before it.

See how easily you did this?

Quit for today – see you tomorrow!

Day 2 – Take a memo

You need a notebook or a new word processing document open on your computer, because now you can brainstorm!

Ideas will now start flowing out of you and you'll need a place to record them. You may remember facts, quotes, insights, people, places, things… it doesn't matter!

1	**2**	3	4	5	6	7

Now you must get them down on paper or into your word-processing document so that you can start organizing them into a sequence.

You see your mind has been given a target.

You told it you want to write a book... a specific book as outlined in your mission statement and that you want to do it in only a few days!

Like a robot or a computer your mind will now bubble up ideas that you may want to include in your book. Simply keep track of them.

You don't do any actual "writing" at this point, just jot down keywords so you can recall the material later.

You might remember a terrific story that you want to include in your book to illustrate a principle. Rather than writing out the story just scribble out a few key words to help anchor the story in your mind.

You might also get a sense of direction for your book. If an idea occurs to you write it down.

If some sense of a pattern in or for the book comes to you, make a note of it.

If you feel the urge to write out the table of contents do it!

If you feel like doing some research at the library or online then do it.

If nothing comes to mind, still no problem!

The process still works on a "below conscious" level, but if you find troubles with your brainstorming session, do this to stimulate your creative juices.

Take a sheet of paper and sketch out the cover of your ebook. This will allow you to visualize what the front cover of the book will look like and help your mind to get a picture of the result you want to achieve, along with a lot of fun!

No matter how crazy, wild, or outrageous – think of anything!

Brainstorm the title.

Think of the picture you want on the front.

What colors do you see?

Don't think too hard – just think from your heart!

If that doesn't get you started try this...

By the way – I use the following method not only to get my head straight and for ideas to flow out of me like someone busted the top off a fire hydrant – I also use it to get myself so motivated to write the material that I often finish my project in a matter of a couple days!

This powerful technique will get you moving!

One of our friends, Yanik Silver, gave a suggestion to me one time that I used to make literally tens of thousands of dollars with more fun writing than I ever dreamed possible.

Write the Sales Letter First!

Go ahead and write the sales letter you will use to sell your ebook – before you ever write the book!

The single most successful marketing technique on the Internet uses a two page web site to sell just about anything. The first page, a sales letter and the second page, a simple order form where you take credit card payments.

Rather than trying to create the book and then write the sales letter – simply reverse the process!

Write the sales letter first and make it totally compelling! Go all out with the bullets and guarantees and all the awesome benefits someone will get from reading this book.

Whip yourself into a frenzy listing all the things that people will learn and all the benefits they will receive – the FREE bonuses they'll get – all the life changing things they will receive as a result of reading your ebook!

Use lots of bullets and descriptive text about all the wonderful things contained in your ebook!

Write it so that *nobody* in your niche target market in their right mind could say no to your incredible offer.

The great thing about this exercise – once you write this totally inspiring and compelling sales letter, you simply go back and create the ebook based on the sales letter!

The sales letter outlines all the great stuff in the book and in the process it totally focuses your mind and gets you completely motivated to get to work on the project.

Even without starting the ebook yet, play with possibilities and make up what you think it should include. Write that sales letter in a persuasive irresistible way and put in whatever you think will make people buy the ebook.

Blow your own mind! It doesn't matter at this point if you know how you will do this, just write a killer letter and your mind will figure out how to create what you laid out beforehand.

Again, treat this exercise as a brainstorming session – create a sales letter that no reader could resist!

No more activity today, so when you finish take a walk or proceed with the rest of your day.

Day 3 – The Race Begins

Better open up your notebook and grab your pencil or limber up your fingers to start typing. Regardless of your feelings at this point get ready to write – because today you will write!

As the shoe people say "just do it!"

Now you may feel a little skeptical at the moment or you may feel a bit of apprehension, but I promise an easy process if you just relax and learn to go with the flow.

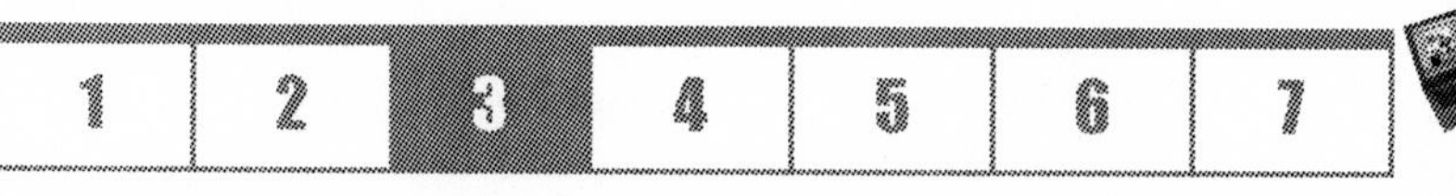

Many "master" writers use this secret in writing a first draft – ready?

- Don't edit ...
- Don't go back...
- DON'T stop!

Keep your hand moving, your mind focused and your fingers moving across the keyboard or moving the pen across the page – it's that simple!

People who say "writing is hard" or "writing is a pain" usually do something that we must insist you don't do. They *edit* as they write – **you must not edit as you write.**

People who get stuck do so because they listen to the little internal voice in their head that says things like "You don't know what you're doing!" Tell that little voice to take a hike... for now.

Tell the little voice inside your head it can come back later and help you edit the book

But right now it's important to get your thoughts down on paper so that you get something to work with. Consider it as a rough draft, but once you get it down then you can edit it.

When you begin writing just keep going. Don't stop... don't edit... just write!

Most importantly – don't judge your work at this point. You'll want to look at what you have written and make judgments about it.

You'll constantly ask yourself questions like:

- "Does this make sense?"
- "Did I do it right?"
- "Will anyone believe me?"
- "Do I know what I'm talking about?"

Just write it!

Is something pops in your mind – write it down. If you need to find out someone's name or a date or a bit of information DON'T STOP to find it out, just make little note in parentheses and keep going. You can fill in the blanks later.

Continue to write no matter what. You must focus no matter what you hear in your mind – KEEP WRITING! Keep your hands moving.

Think of editing and writing as two different functions. You can't do both at the same time with any skill.

Put your pen on page one of your notebook or your fingers on the keyboard and start moving. Write whatever comes to mind. Write nonsense... write gibberish... write whatever... just keep writing.

This incredibly good news may shock you...

Because of your focusing statement and letting your mind incubate on the subject of your ebook, whatever you write will allow you to create your ebook. In other words, you won't write gibberish or nonsense because you already set up a target and now you will keep moving towards it.

Today spend at least two to four hours writing nonstop. You can divide it up into full or half hour sessions or you can even do a series of 20-minute sessions – Your choice!

You can even spend the entire day working on your book.

Now you and I both know you can't write an entire book in two hours. But you can certainly write an entire first draft in a couple of days if you devote six to eight hours a day to it for a couple of days in a row.

So if you really want to write an entire ebook within the seven days, today, tomorrow and the next day you need to write, write, and write in every spare moment you can find.

But who knows, you might even get the entire ebook done today if you start early in the morning and stop only long enough to use the bath-

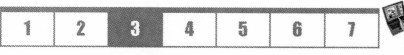

room and grab a quick bite to eat. If you really go at it all day nonstop, you could turn out an ebook-length first draft in as fast as one day.

Remember, writing communicates, so it may help if you pretend to write your book as a letter to a friend. This will help keep your writing focused, friendly and on target. As you write, keep your friend in mind, so you make sure to explain yourself in a clear, easy-to-follow way.

Now take your turn!

Now the pedal hits the metal and the rubber meets the road – where writing your ebook really begins. Put down this book and start writing… and remember to have fun, smell the roses, and enjoy the process of discovery!

Day 4 & 5 – Keep Writing

Keep up the momentum!

Continue with your writing sessions and write nonstop. Break up your day and write in 20 and 30 minute segments... just keep writing!

Again, don't edit or stop or judge your writing.

Your first draft, while rough, will probably exceed your expectations. While you write, you can't possibly clearly judge your material – don't even try! Just keep writing and suspend judgment for now.

You may feel like you're writing the ending first or the middle last.

You may feel your opening stinks.

You may feel like you haven't communicated … it doesn't matter!

You'll straighten it all out later. Your sole purpose, keep your hand moving and the words flowing no matter what – **just do it!**

No big deal if you truly let go and write what comes to mind. Write from the depths of your own heart and soul about something that truly interests you, where you can get really passionate. You just need to write your passionate thoughts down and get them on paper.

When you write without editing, the inner struggle most people feel when they try to write something, almost magically disappears.

Keep writing and by the end of day 5 you'll complete your first draft!

You might find it hard to read and imagine as a finished ebook, but trust me it will form the basis of your ebook. Only two more days worth of work and you're home free.

Day 6 – Bring Back the "Little Voice" – It's time to Edit

Now you can edit your book.

First, organize the book.

You might find the beginning buried somewhere in the rough drafts. Pull it out and put it on top. Do the same for any other sections – put them where you think they belong.

Trust your gut… you probably know how you could best reorganize the ebook, so go with your feelings.

Once you think you've organized it, move on the second step

Second, throw away anything the ebook doesn't need.

You'll find it hard to drop the wonderful words you worked so hard on the last few days, but think of your focusing statement. If any material doesn't help you achieve that purpose – drop that material.

For example, if you tell a story that doesn't in any way apply to what you want to accomplish, drop the story.

Third, go through the pages and tighten up what you wrote.

If you left out names, dates or facts, now add them.

If you got too wordy see if you can tighten up your text.

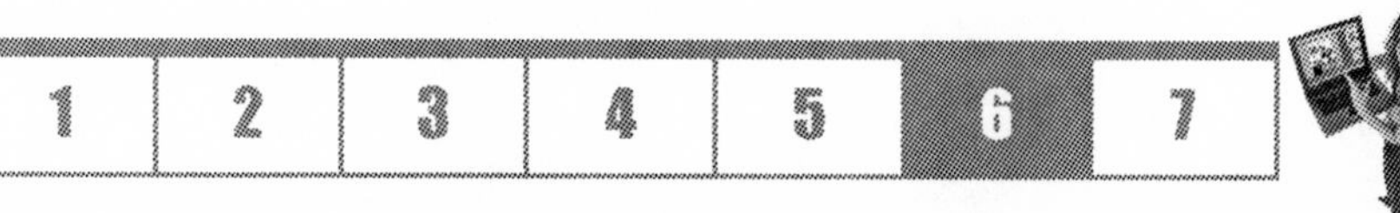

If you seem to use one word a lot, break out your thesaurus and see if you can find another word that says the same thing, without making it sound like you just try to use "big" words.

Fourth, consider deleting the opening and ending sections.

The start and finish of your ebook usually – but not always – contain weak areas. Often times writers will start writing something before they start saying something.

Look carefully at your opening and your conclusion to make sure they say what they should – especially when you take into consideration your focusing statement.

*Drop anything you see, if it seems your book will work better without it.

Fifth, see if you can break up your text into smaller sub-sections.

Traditional books divide into chapters, however in ebooks people want to find information quickly. Often they will buy your ebook because of just one section, not because they want to read the entire thing.

Dividing up your book in bite-sized chunks will make it easier for your customers to read, especially while reading directly from their computer screens.

Split the chapters into bite-size sections, each with its own heading and lots of bullets and subheadings. See if you can do this for your manuscript, to help make the reader's experience easier on the eyes as well as the mind.

NOTE: Creating your ebook with lots of sub sections, headers and bullets will also increase the overall perceived length of the ebook because this increases white space.

Doing this kills two birds with one stone – your book appears longer and worth the money people paid and also makes it much more readable and enjoyable for them.

You actually do your readers a service by formatting your ebook this way.

Spend the day going through your material organizing, polishing, editing and perfecting it.

How to Get FREE Editing Services

Don't make editing such a big deal – just do the best you can on your own and then stop.

When you get as far as you can, I want you to contact at least six friends, colleagues or peers in your industry and ask them to review your ebook. When they say yes email (or regular "snail mail") it to them and invite their comments.

Avoid the vicious trap most aspiring authors fall into – these people want to help you! You get free editing services that often times cost thousands of dollars – so take what these people tell you with a grain of salt and act extremely grateful for the help.

In other words... don't get insulted – act grown-up about it!

If one person says something seems wrong, points out an area that might need improvement or asks a question about the book, you can either agree with it or disagree with it. Remember, you invited constructive feedback from people who should care about you. I doubt very seriously you will send it out to people who would make malicious comments about your ebook.

If all six people tell you something seems wrong, point out an area that needs improvement or ask the same question, then you need to jump up, get excited and say "Hey, I need to address this. I can improve and make the book even better here!"

I must emphasize again that no one who knows you or cares about you will say mean things to you – they want to help!

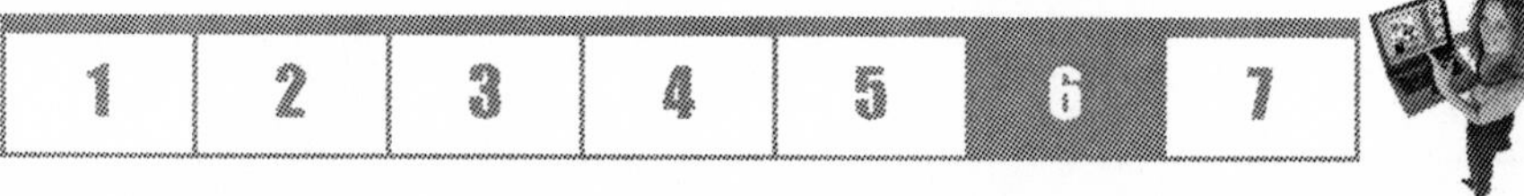

You should accept their editing help, whether it's asking questions about your ideas, correcting spelling mistakes, questions about formatting, questions about stories – whatever.

Accept and receive feedback – in fact, you want this constructive feedback, even if it seems negative.

You want this kind of feedback ***before*** a whole group of people pay you $20... $30... $40 or more for your ebook and all of a sudden some glaring mistake comes up that causes everybody to ask for their money back.

What a nightmare!

Ask them politely to edit the book and let them know they can say whatever they want and you won't take their comments personally.

Once your friends respond, then edit and revise your book again.

- Does it look like a good ebook to you?
- Do you feel satisfied?
- Does it live up to the intention you set out for it on day one?
- If not, what does the book need to finish up?

Once you finish then move on to the next step – Day Seven – where you publish your ebook in a form that will make it universally available to everyone on the Internet – whether they use a PC or Mac – read the subject of the next chapter very carefully!

Day 7 – Publishing Your eBook for the Web!

Note: *A really smart person might combine all of these steps and write an ebook in one weekend. Regardless of how you get yourself down the trail to this point, I hope you see it as entirely possible (in fact a lot more preferable and less painful than taking months to do it) to plan and write your ebook in less than seven days and then publish it for distribution on the Worldwide Web.*

1	2	3	4	5	6	7

Day 7 – How to Publish Your eBook for the Web

Face it! Not everybody you sell a book to will own the latest and greatest computer the form and format of your book will not match up with their machine, you will only accomplish a return of the product or reverse charges on their credit card.

Two primary methods will physically publish your ebook, but, in my opinion, one works much better than the other.

The first way, not my choice, uses an HTML ebook compiler program.

We don't recommend these programs, not because they don't work. They actually do work very well except for the fact that you can only sell your information to people who own a PC with the right software on it. MAC owners can't use the types of files these compilers create (.exe files) so you immediately limit the number of people who can purchase your ebook right off the bat.

Now you might want to use an ebook compiler that uses HTML documents as the pages of the book to tie in existing web pages and make them look like part of the book. Since an HTML ebook compiler can also access web pages if the person is connected to Internet at the time of reading the book, you can make your ebook appear larger than reality.

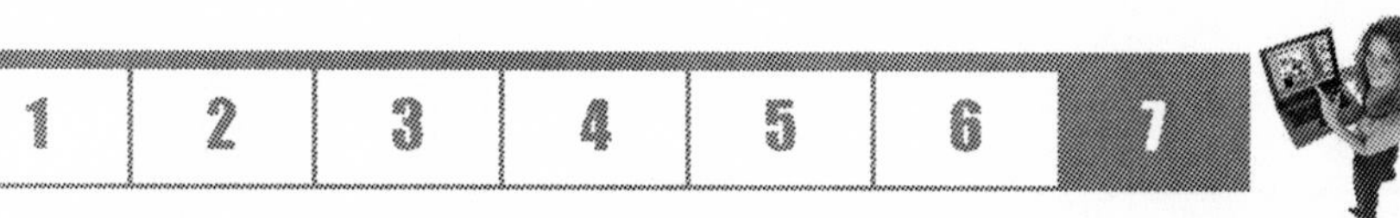

But a reader not connected to the web won't see parts of the book. You risk a refund any time someone must think in order to view your material.

For these reasons we recommend using PDF documents viewed through the FREE Adobe Acrobat Reader.

Because:

1. PDF documents are universally readable by any computer with the Adobe Acrobat Reader installed. Adobe Acrobat Reader is a free program. If you are reading this ebook then you obviously have the Reader program and can use it.

2. The PDF documents you create will look EXACTLY the same no matter what type of screen or computer people use. This is especially important if you have a lot of graphs and charts and other illustrations. That won't have a consistent / authentic look if you created them in an HTML ebook.

3. Adobe Acrobat itself operates as a very stable program. Rarely will you find anyone who can't open your document or get problems reading or printing it. This cuts the time on any customer service or technical support work you might do – a key advantage when you start selling a bunch of books.

You can use a couple of different ways to convert your word-processing documents into PDF format for viewing in Adobe Acrobat Reader. However, if you want to create more than just a basic PDF document that, for example, includes live web links, you must buy the full Adobe Acrobat program, or hire someone to create the document for you… no way around it!

But look at it this way – if you really want to make it big in the world of online "e" publishing – invest in Adobe Acrobat as the single most important and wisest money you can spend.

But we also know a FREE way to convert your documents, using a little known resource, available to help any aspiring e-publisher create basic PDF documents in a snap without the need to buy the full version of the Adobe Acrobat software or hire outside help.

Publish Basic PDF's FREE Online

The easiest way to publish your file as a basic PDF – first prepare your ebook, report or other document in a word processor such as Microsoft Word or WordPerfect and make sure you fully proof read and edit the final version.

*The reason for carefully finalizing your document comes from the fact that once you convert the file to a PDF you can't edit the text in that PDF without owning the Adobe Acrobat program – so make sure you get ready to publish before proceeding.

With the file ready to convert, log on to https://createpdf.adobe.com, where the title of the page should say "Create Adobe PDF Online".

Click on "Try it for free" and complete the short sign up process.

Adobe will email you your sign up confirmation as well as your user name and password.

Once you activate your account you can log onto their site and convert up to five documents for free. You may have to split your documents into smaller parts if converting the whole file exceeds the 10 minute conversion time limit on the free service.

Follow these detailed, step-by-step instructions for using the free PDF maker at Adobe.com

Once you log onto the site with your user name and password, follow these instructions to create a basic PDF.

Step 1. Choose a file to convert

To choose the file you want to convert, click the "Browse" button. In the File Upload window, click on the file you want to convert to Adobe

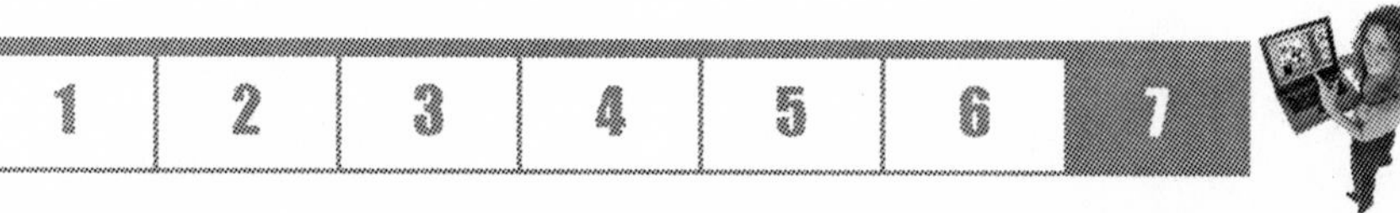

PDF, and click "Open". If you wrote your ebook in a word processor just go to that file on your hard drive and select it.

If you didn't create your ebook in a word processor, the following lists all the document types the Adobe site will convert into PDF format:

Microsoft® Office:

Word (.doc), Publisher (.pub), PowerPoint (.ppt), Excel (.xls), Rich Text Format (.rtf), Text (.txt)

Adobe Formats:

Illustrator® (.ai), InDesign™ (.indd), FrameMaker® (.fm), PageMaker® (.pm, .pm6, .p65), Photoshop® (.psd)

Corel WordPerfect Office Formats:

WordPerfect (.wpd)

Adobe PostScript® Formats:

PostScript (.ps, .prn), Encapsulated PostScript (.eps)

Image Formats:

Windows bitmap (.bmp), GIF (.gif), JPEG (.jpg), PCX (.pcx), PNG (.png), RLE (.rle), TIFF (.tif)

Web pages:

.htm, .html, .shtml

Note: In Netscape Communicator, the File upload window only shows HTML files. To see all file types, select All Files (*.*) from the Files Type drop down menu.

Step 2. Select your "optimization settings"

Create Adobe PDF Online provides predefined optimization options for Web, eBook, Screen, Print, and Press applications.

In this case, you should use the "eBook Settings" option, unless you are already highly familiar with Adobe Acrobat in which case you probably already own the program or can access it and don't need this section.

The "eBook Settings" does the following for your document:

- Creates an Adobe PDF file small enough for Web distribution.
- Embedding all fonts used in the document preserves the fidelity of the document.
- Images are down-sampled to 150 dpi, which will allow users to zoom in for greater detail on the screen while offering reasonable print quality.
- Colors convert to sRGB for consistent color reproduction across different printers.
- Adds thumbnails of the pages, which you can use to navigate through the document.

All this "mumbo jumbo" means that your ebook will get the best settings for delivering off a website and allowing people to easily read your ebook on their computers or print it off on their laser or inkjet printer.

Step 3. Set Security Options if needed

You can limit access to Adobe PDF files by giving the files passwords and restricting certain features such as printing and editing.

A PDF file can require a password to open the document as well as require a password to change the password!

To add security to a PDF file, click set security options and set the following options:

In the Security dialog box, specify any password protection you want:

In the "User Password" text box, enter the password users must enter before they can open the file.

In the "Master Password" text box, enter the password users must enter before they can set or change any security options.

You should not use the same password in both boxes. In most cases your delivery will stay secure so you should probably NOT use this password setting except for a very good reason.

Adding a password creates one more potential stumbling block for people trying to read your ebook and you should probably avoid it.

Next you can "Set Permissions" using the checkboxes:

"No Printing" prevents users from printing the file – you should NOT use this option without a valid reason. Many people print off ebooks to read offline.

"No Changing the Document" prevents users from making any changes to the document – we recommend this setting.

"No Content Copying or Extraction" prevents users from copying text and graphics and pasting them into their own publications – we also recommend this.

"No Adding or Changing Comments or Form Fields" prevents users from adding or changing these areas – we also recommend this.

Once you make all your selections click "Set".

NOTE: If you selected the password protection option, a Password confirmation dialog will display. Enter the correct password, and click "Save".

Step 4. Now you can get your PDF file.... (Delivery Method)

Choose one of the delivery methods from the dropdown menu:

Convert now in Web browser – Leave your computer connected to the Internet and your browser open, and the site will display your PDF file as soon as it finishes the conversion. The conversion process usually takes only a few minutes.

E-mail the link to my file – If you don't want to sit online and wait, then the site will e-mail you a URL where you can pick up your file. The site will only store your file for 72 hours after creating it – so don't sit around and not get the file.

E-mail the file as an attachment – Select this option if you want your PDF file sent to you as an e-mail attachment.

Final Notes About PDF's

PDF offers the file of choice for ebook publishers, not only for its stability, but also for the fact that it runs on just about any computer and operating system you can think of. Except for a VERY good reason not to, you should plan on publishing your ebook for the web in the PDF format.

One of PDF's great features centers on your ability to not only share information, but to protect it as well. With PDF documents you can limit what people do with your written material by restricting whether or not they can highlight text, copy and paste or even print the document.

Another great thing about publishing and PDF is that you can also include "live" web links, where you include web addresses. Let's say you had some affiliate programs you signed up for and you want to refer people to someone else's web site for more information and get paid if they buy. This feature alone can make you a significant amount of money.

> *NOTE: In order to take advantage of this web link feature, however, you must purchase the Adobe Acrobat program or find someone who owns it and pay that person to help you.*

Alternative Publishing Option – "Print on Demand" Publishers

Print on demand publishing, a new process, allows ebook authors to enter the world of offline publishing without the heartache, time and money expense of finding an agent and then wooing a publisher.

Print on demand publishers offer a wide variety of services, but basically they store your book electronically in a "super computer" hooked up to a high-speed printing press. When someone comes to their website – whether a consumer or a buyer for an offline bookstore – and wants to purchase your book, they either receive your book as an ebook or the publisher's machinery spits out however many hard copies of the books they need.

The beauty of print on demand lets the publisher produce single copies of the book and everybody still makes money!

Now your profit margin with a print on demand publisher lessens quite a bit over your selling the book yourself strictly as an ebook. But a print on demand publisher can also give you a lot more flexibility in delivering your

publication. Like it or not, a lot of people still want a hard copy of the book and will pay extra in order to get it.

This news story ran in several publications and newspapers across the country about how Joe used a print on demand publisher to launch his newest book, "Spiritual Marketing".

Internet Changes the Face of Book Publishing

The fact that a friend of mine recently published a new book came as no surprise since he has already published about ten others. However, as I dug deeper into the story I realized he was using the Internet exclusively to publish, print and sell his book.

A growing trend among authors, even established writers with dozens of books to their credit, involves using "print-on-demand" publishers, email and websites to sell just as many if not more books faster than by traditional publishing and marketing methods.

The story about the how the book has been published and marketed rates as impressive and innovative as the actual subject of the book. The writer, Joe Vitale, has written books for such organizations as the American Marketing Association and the American Management Association.

His latest book "Spiritual Marketing" takes a spiritual, almost metaphysical, approach to accomplishing your business and personal objectives. Since the book approaches operating your life and business in more direct fashion, it seems natural that the production and marketing of the book should also stray from the beaten path.

Joe decided to use a "print-on-demand" publisher, 1st Books Library (www.1stbooks.com). Most people expect that authors cash in on lucrative book deals and fat royalty checks. The realities of traditional publishing come as a shock when they discover it takes years to get a book published and the giant publishing houses do little to market a book.

If the author wants book sales then it is up to them to hit the trail marketing the book. Publishers print books – authors sell books!

Advancements in computer and printing technology have made the miracle of "print-on-demand" publishing possible. With print-on-demand a book doesn't get printed until a customer places an order, thus eliminating the risk most publishers take by printing thousands of books that may or may not sell.

Also, print-on-demand publishers enable authors to distribute their work in electronic form as "eBooks" customers download and print right from their computer screen.

As proven by the Harry Potter phenomenon, "word of mouth" advertising represents the best way to sell books. Traditional book marketing involves the hit-and-miss book signing circuit. Joe took a different approach.

He emailed everyone he knew or did business with, told them briefly about his book, and then told them they could go to Amazon.com or 1stBooks.com to order a copy. Just that one email has sparked book sales all over the world as people read the book and tell their friends.

Even though the book has only been available commercially for a couple of months, Joe has sold hundreds and this initial success has even led to discussions with a famous offline publisher.

If you could use a lift in your personal or business life, Joe Vitale's innovative book, "Spiritual Marketing" is well worth picking up. Plus, when you think about the exciting and ground-breaking process that brings the book to your computer screen or front door it makes the whole purchase that much more exciting.

Source: www.thenetreporter.com

Another story recently ran about two authors who use a combination of ebook publishing, print on demand and traditional publicity tactics to not only sell books, but break into the traditional world of publishing as well.

The Next "Harry Potter"?

When local authors, Roger P. Myers & Albert E. Herbert, Jr., set out to write their book, "The Quest", they were already experienced hands at using print on demand publishers. Now, as they promote their epic adventure, the two authors try to bridge the completely different worlds of online and offline book publishing to bring their tale of wizards and "illusionists" in the distant past to the readers of the present.

Myers and Herbert have chosen to use the services of online print on demand publisher, Xlibris (www.Xlibris.com), rather than go the often frustrating, costly and heart-breaking route of finding a traditional literary agent and publisher.

The authors have found that having a completed manuscript, hard-bound and in-hand gets them a lot more attention, not only from the public eager to purchase their book, but also from literary agencies.

The pair currently has the book with a major agency and are awaiting a reply.

While they wait, however, the authors are not sitting on their keyboards waiting for the world to beat a path to their door. More and more authors have discovered that, even if you are lucky enough to find a publisher, traditional publishing houses do little if anything to promote their books.

The pair has taken the very traditional approach of sending out promotional post cards to several mailing lists as well as sending evaluation copies of the book to media contacts for review. The two have discovered that part of the title "Best Selling

Author" includes the word selling – and that's what this pair intends to do.

Myers and Herbert offer advice for new authors from experience gained through several books and years of trial and learning. "We have been very successful using the online book publishers, Xlibris and iUniverse (www.iuniverse.com). We chose this publishing route because we were unsuccessful in getting an agent just by sending in a manuscript."

The two further advise, though print on demand and electronic publishing open doors closed by traditional avenues, there are added responsibilities placed on the author. "If you have something worthwhile you want to share, we would go with the POD (print on demand) books.

But remember: You are your own editor. These services do not edit your manuscript. So, be thorough and make sure everything is perfect before submitting your manuscript for printing."

Myers and Herbert have several other books besides "The Quest" to their credit and have watched the face of print on demand publishing change and grow over the last few years.

The basic services of Xlibris used to come free of charge, however now the basic package costs $200. The two caution however that this increase in price is a paltry amount when compared to the cost of "vanity" press publishing which used to represent a self-publishing author's only alternative to finding a traditional publisher.

Though their publishing represent the latest in printing and delivery, the authors will hold a very traditional book signing at William and Mary's Bookstore on Jamestown Road in Williamsburg, VA Sunday, August 12, from 1:00 to 3:00.

Source: www.thenetreporter.com

Though we cannot recommend a specific service, you may want to consider one of these print on demand publishers:

www.xlibris.com

www.iuniverse.com

www.1stbooks.com

You can also find a bunch of print on demand publishing sites with more information by going to **www.Yahoo.com** and searching for "print-on-demand."

Notes about dealing with print on demand (or any other electronic) publishers or bookstores:

1. Make sure you retain the rights to your book. Don't let someone tie up your publishing rights in case you find a better or more profitable way to market and sell your book.

2. Make sure you understand exactly how much you make off the sales of the books and compare the royalties offered between various publishers.

3. Read over any contracts thoroughly. Don't sign anything you don't understand or don't feel comfortable with completely. An attorney should look over anything that looks odd – or just move on to another publisher. Many print on demand publishers pop up and you can choose from a lot of them.

4. Don't get swayed by promises of marketing help and distribution. These print on demand publishers will list your books with registries and make it available to book stores – but ultimately you market the book. The same holds true in the traditional publishing world. Publishers print books – authors promote books.

5. Make sure you understand exactly what you do and don't get for the money you spend with a print on demand publisher. Sometimes

spending more doesn't mean you'll get better results. Remember the whole point here – make more money than you spend!

6. A possibility exists that offline bookstores and other distribution sources will pick up your book through a print on demand publisher, so make sure you carefully compare prices and services between them before signing with anyone.

7. Carefully read and make sure you understand the submission process before you begin. Mistakes here can cost you time and money.

8. **CAREFULLY EDIT YOUR BOOK!** Print on demand publishers will not edit your book – so any typos, misquotes, failure to credit sources, etc. lie with you and will show up in the book. No editor will save you this time around!

The BIG Breakthrough

Writing versus Editing

One of the two biggest hurdles you will encounter in writing your ebook in seven days – overcoming your desire to edit your text as you write.

(I'll tell you the other major stumbling block in a few minutes.)

If you tried to build a house you would find it very difficult to build that house and put up each piece (board-by-board and brick-by-brick) and paint and spackle as you went along.

When a builder puts up a house, first they put up the frame, then they put in the floor, then the roof, then plumbing and electrical and finally they paint and put in the trim and finishing work.

You can't build any house in a reasonable period of time any other way!

While writing a book –a regular book or an ebook – a little voice in the back of your head keeps talking to you. It says everything from "you can't write" to "this doesn't make any sense" to "will anybody buy this" and a whole bunch of other internal dialogue that does nothing more than slow down the process of writing.

Visualize yourself as a little kid trying to build a sand castle at the beach.

Before you could start shaping the castle you first piled up a huge mountain of sand and then cleared away everything that didn't look like a

sand castle. You piled up the sand, shaped it, molded it and finally you wound up with a sculpture.

But until you piled up the sand you couldn't do one darn thing!

This also happens with writing versus editing.

Before you can edit... **you must write.**

In order to write... **you must start writing.**

Now I know this point sounds overly simplistic... but in order to get your ebook to where you can edit it, you first must put it down on paper or into the computer.

So when you begin writing you must disconnect the little voice that will criticize, question, and slow you down.

Trust yourself that you really know something and you will prove it!

You could not think of the idea for your ebook in the first place, without the capacity to either write it straight out or come up with the outline / framework of the book and then research the topic. If you must research the topic, you will find all the material, facts and supporting documentation that will provide a valuable service to the people who eventually purchase your ebook.

Stop worrying... start writing!

So during the early days of the seven day process of writing your ebook you need to make a conscious effort to blow through the material you're creating as quickly as possible.

In a flurry of energy and effort, don't give the little voice of doubt any room to slow you down or stop you. This little voice of doubt truly stops more people from finishing (yet alone even beginning) an ebook.

What a shame, because a great ebook could help them not only to make a significant amount of money, but to gain the fabulous feelings that come from creating something that renders extreme value for large numbers of people – plus rewards of personal prestige, recognition and professional accomplishment in the process.

So just like the sand castle, once you create the pile of raw text to serve as the building blocks of your ebook, you can begin the process of editing and polishing your ebook.

But until you pile up the text you can't edit! Plus, remember, you don't worry about editing the book all by yourself – your friends will help you!

So stop feeling the pressure of "not good enough" and just speak from your heart and give all the material, knowledge and information you can. Then organize it and polish it later on in the editing process.

If you adopt this mind set we feel certain you can write your own book length manuscript within the seven day program we outline. Then take that manuscript, publish it, and go on your way to creating something that brings you personal and financial reward for many years to come.

"A Journey of a 1000 Miles Begins with One Step"

The other major stumbling block people run into when it comes to writing, creating, and editing their ebook, comes down to seeing the project as much larger and imposing than in reality.

I think this goes back to high school and college (and maybe even grade school) when teachers assigned books to read in English class. Those books seemed large and imposing and, at that time, most of us could barely write and turn in five page papers – let alone think ourselves capable of writing something 50, 100, even 200 pages long.

We want to give you a few tips that will help you to break this ebook project down into a more manageable process that you can eagerly attack – rather than run away from it (even on a subconscious level) thinking you can't create something this big!

Some of this material may overlap with the seven day method and other parts of the book, but we want to make sure you completely understand these VERY valuable points!

3 Sure-Fire Tips to Whip Out an eBook in Record Time

First Tip – Write a letter

Write the material as a letter to a person you know, love, trust and really want to help.

Writing letters is a "snap"! Writing books can be "hard"! So write letters instead of book chapters.

Think of your ebook not as a book, but as a series of letters written to someone that you cared deeply for. Pretend you really want to explain a certain subject or topic to them and do it in a way you know they'll understand.

Lead them down the path of understanding the subject you write about, so when they get to the end, you know they found all the tools they need to succeed at whatever you want to teach.

This means that you just divide up the information you want to convey into a bunch of small subjects. Outline each of them, either on paper or in a word processor, and then explain each section in the form of a letter.

You know how to write a letter, don't you?

Sure you do!

Remember…

You would first introduce the problem, explain the solution and then draw the conclusions the person should get from that particular letter.

NOTE: When I use this technique I find it helpful to get a picture of someone I know and love and put in front of me for a pretend dialogue with this person. It helps me anticipate their questions and concerns. I then answer those questions and address those concerns in a warm, comfortable, almost conversational tone.

If you really want to publish your own ebook then you have what it takes to explain your topic to someone else in the form of letters. This excellent method quickly communicates information to your readers so they can get what they need from your ebook.

Second tip – Make a List

Give 10 reasons for making something, doing something, or understanding something.

Lists let you easily express anything on your mind.

David Letterman's popular "Top-10" lists have even been gathered into books.

Start thinking in the form of top-10 lists.

Focus on 10 items you want to communicate.

Create an outline in a word processor that covers all the major topics that you want to cover in your ebook.

Then take that outline and expand each point by adding two points underneath it. At this stage of the process it does not matter if you use complete sentences. You only want to organize your ideas in an orderly fashion so you can lead someone logically through your information.

Next take all of these sub-points and add two more points to each of them.

For example: Let's say you started out with 10 main points and then added two sub-points to each. This means you now have 30 points, issues, ideas or thoughts you want to communicate.

This usually gives enough information to create what we would consider a "report" length publication of between 20 and 30 pages.

If you go back and create two more points, ideas or thoughts on each of your 10 original main points and the 20 additional sub-points, you created 90 total ideas, points, stories or issues to cover!

With this outline you can now write a paragraph or two about each item and, using the techniques in the chapter on formatting your ebook, you can turn out a very nice ebook quickly.

You can easily turn a document of 90 to 180 paragraphs in length into an ebook, especially if you add some collateral material, such as:

- Website links
- Expert interviews
- Bonus material
- Guest articles
- Case studies

This "list" method can turn out an ebook-length publication in a matter of days – guaranteed!

So stop looking at your ebook as this great big mountain you must climb.

Instead look at it as a series of steps that you can easily conquer and just do them in order.

We see people use this technique (ourselves included) to create book-length publications of between 75 and 200 pages in length in a matter of only two days.

Third Tip – Tell Stories

We use stories to make sense of our lives and they give people something real, to relate to their own life situations.

Give examples of your own experiences and how you came to do something or understand something. Use stories that illustrate the techniques you want to teach about in your ebook – especially when writing a "how to" ebook.

Stories help you to expand your points and bring information home to your readers in a way they can use much more readily than if you just throw facts, dates and advice at them without giving real world scenarios for them to relate to their own lives.

Physically Getting Your Text on Paper

If you remember, one of the sub headlines for this ebook said "*How to write and publish your own outrageously profitable ebook in only seven days – even if you can't write, can't type and failed high school English class!*"

In this section we'll cover a couple of different ways to get your text into your computer so you can publish it into ebook form – even if you can't type.

Special note: Don't expect a free lunch!

We don't know of a free way to get your information down on paper or into your computer if you don't do it. You either type it or you hire somebody to type it for you.

But alternatives to the traditional sit down at the keyboard and bang the thing out and developing carpal tunnel disease, do exist!

Hey – we understand – we don't want you reliving those nightmare experiences of doing your term paper the night before, and running through white-out like you got paid to use it! We want a pleasant experience for everyone… especially you!

"Even if you failed English class"...

Now in the chapter on the "The 7 Day eBook Writing Method" we explain how to get free editing services for your ebook – so even if you failed high school English class you can turn out a nice publication.

If you ask nicely, at least six other people (who probably did pass English class) will help you get your text into a form and format you would feel comfortable selling and for eager customers to read.

So don't sweat that part – nobody cares how well you did or didn't do in English class. That happened a long time ago!

"Even if you can't write"...

Writing, and the traditional rules about "good" writing, don't really apply when it comes to creating a "how to" ebook or any other "information product".

Traditional writing rules tell you never to use the words I, me, my, you your, yours and so on because they sound "too familiar".

Bull!

When trying to communicate information to someone in a way they can immediately grasp and implement (for which they pay you), then a conversational writing style works best.

Imagine the person sitting right in front of you and you tell this person how to accomplish a certain task or understand a certain concept and how it can help them.

"If you can talk – you can write!"

If you can talk and explain things in simple, step-by-step terms – you can write in a style that creates a very effective "how to" publication.

If you can talk and explain your ideas and thoughts about a subject then don't worry any more!

You can write!

… and you *will* write in a way that helps people – just remember why they want to buy your ebook in the first place!

How Summer School Changed Jim's Life

At age 15 years, my parents made me go to summer school.

Now I always got pretty good grades so the thought of going to school during the summer never occurred to me, until one day I came home from the neighborhood pool and my mother informed me that she had enrolled me in summer school.

After I got over my initial shock and could speak again, I asked her what class I would take.

She gleefully informed me that she had signed me up for typing class.

Typing Class?!

Imagine back when you were 15 years old. Think about summer vacation and looking forward to a couple of months of friends, swimming, baseball, tennis and videogames.

Now imagine your mom informs you that you will go to school for 2 months in the middle of the summer to learn how to type.

Oh the agony!

So every day I trudged to school – and to make matters worse I lived right down the street from the school, so I could walk past the pool and listen to all my friends enjoying themselves while I went to "typing" class.

"Hey Edwards, have fun at typing class!" they would all shout with fiendish delight as they frolicked in the pool

The worst summer of my life – or so I thought at the time.

15 years later that typing class actually turned into one of the most significant accomplishments of my life.

"Why" you ask?

Because my ability to type enabled me to quickly create the information products and ebooks that changed my life – especially from a financial standpoint.

As it turns out I actually "lucked out" with a mother who would send me to summer school to learn to type… thanks mom!

However, **most people can't type with any speed** and their fingers can't keep up with their brain – so most people can't compose at the keyboard.

If you fit this mold we can present some alternatives for you.

However, one last word about typing…

If you know how to type at all (even a little bit), then get your book into the computer for electronic publication quickly by sitting down and composing at the keyboard.

Sit down and just start typing!

As ideas flow and your body gets into the process your whole being starts to focus on the task at hand – i.e. getting this text into your computer!

As you get into that "flow" your typing speed will naturally increase and, in some cases, increase dramatically.

Even if you can only type 30 words a minute (a fairly slow rate) and can only type for 20 minute sessions – that still means you can turn out over one full page of single spaced text (500 to 600 words) every 20 minutes.

In the section on the formatting your ebook we explain how one single space typewritten page can turn into as much as three pages of ebook text.

So even if you can only type 30 words a minute you can turn out the text you need to create the majority of your ebook in just a couple of days.

So if you can type even a little bit – sit down and start typing.

However, if you can't type at all, then do this:

"Even if you can't type"...

Two Alternatives to Typing

Voice Recognition Software

Look at one of the most exciting developments for computers in the last few years – the growth of inexpensive voice recognition software.

In 1997 I bought my first voice recognition software program and quite frankly – it stunk!

However, voice recognition software has come a long way and I recently bought a package from IBM (Via Voice for Windows) that cost only $30.

This software allows you to speak into a microphone and your computer takes your words and turns them into type on the screen. In fact, huge chunks of this ebook came from dictation directly into my computer which I then tightened up in my word processor.

I simply wrote down an outline of the major points and sub-points we wanted to cover in this ebook and stood in my home office and talked about them – imagining that I talked and explained the subjects directly to you.

A "fast" typist can type about 70 words a minute. Most average typists can only do about 30 to 40 words a minute.

However, you can speak at around 200 to 250 words per minute, yet you think at about 450 words per minute

Can you see why your fingers fall behind your brain? Can you see the problem for most people?

This voice recognition software goes beyond AWESOME!

If you can explain your subject or tell a story to someone one-on-one, this software allows you to get it all into your computer, then pull it into your word processor and tighten it up.

Even "hunters and a peckers," when it comes to typing can get all the raw text out of their heads and into the computer very quickly, especially if you just talk about your subject like you were explaining it to a friend.

A word of warning – you can't use this software on some old Pentium 133 computer with 16 MB of RAM! You must use a computer only one or two years old in order to use this software effectively.

I highly recommend that you check out the software package I used – IBM's ViaVoice for Windows Personal Edition. It takes some practice – and it will miss a few words here and there – but the package presents an excellent tool if you take the time to learn how to use it.

Check the next alternative if you can't (or don't want to) type at all – not even one single little bit of typing!

Do what Doctors do…

Doctors used this technique for decades to get large quantities of their thoughts down in written form without taking the time to type them up themselves -or to even write them out by hand.

You can use a transcription service.

You would create a written outline of the major points and sub-points you want to cover and then, instead of dictating into your computer, you would dictate into a tape recorder.

Once you dictate everything into the tape cassette you would simply give it to the tape transcriber and they would type up what you recorded.

Transcription services charge anywhere between 1¢ and 2¢ per word, which means you would pay approximately $5 – 7.50 per type written page, single-spaced with 12 point font.

Now this may sound like a lot of money, but it means that you can dictate 50 pages worth of information and it will cost you $250 for the first draft of your ebook in a couple of days.

After you got the first draft back from the transcription service you would simply print off a copy and make your editing changes in red pen directly on the paper.

Finally, you could hire somebody to make your changes for you in a word processor, format your type, and then publish your document as a PDF.

This option works for the truly hands-off person without the time, desire or ability to do it any other way.

So there you have it – two sure-fire ways to get your text down on paper if you can't type it out yourself directly.

Others exist, such as handwriting recognition pads (mine doesn't work very well) and the like, but voice recognition and dictation work best and fastest.

Formatting Your eBook Text

People read differently from their computer screens and from 8 1/2 by 11 printed sheets of paper than they do from regular or "traditional" book size sheets of paper.

Because of these physical differences – formatting an ebook differs significantly from formatting a book for offline publication.

You must understand this point clearly so you don't publish your ebook as a bunch of single spaced text that fills up entire 8 ½ x 11 pages – this will make it difficult for people to read your material and benefit from it.

Very Important NOTE: If your readers can't easily absorb the information you sold them, you face a high likelihood of getting a return or a credit card "chargeback" and losing money… *not* the goal in writing an ebook!

The "Rules"…

There exist no hard and fast rules as far as the "correct way" to format the text for an ebook. However, a number of good design tips apply, no matter whether you format a flyer, an ebook, a website, a brochure or even a traditional book.

The following tips should help you format the text in your ebook to make it as readable and enjoyable for your audience as possible – and allow them to absorb your information and feel good about their experience with you.

Number 1 – Use lots of white space.

- Now this doesn't mean you only put three paragraphs on a page with triple-spaced text and 2 inch margins on the left and right!
- This means you can use a lot of double spaces to keep the text from running into large blocks that will easily tire your readers' eyes.

Number 2 – Use lots of bullets.

- Bullets act like miniature headlines!
- People will read bullets and absorb information much more easily than from reading long paragraphs.
- Bullets get straight to-the-point, allowing you to convey important aspects of your information quickly.

Number 3 – Don't use 10-point (small) type sizes.

- At a minimum use 12-point type because the bigger type font the easier for people to read it.
- Also, don't go to the other extreme of making all of your type at 18 point so it appears so huge on the screen people can't read it.

Number 4 – Keep it consistent.

- Stay consistent from page to page in the way you format and organize your text.
- Always keep your headlines the same size and in the same alignment on the pages.
    - For example: if your chapter headings use 20 point type centered

on the page, then make every chapter heading 20 point type and centered on the page.

- If your subheads all use 12 point type with round bullets, then keep these subheads consistent throughout the entire ebook.

- Switching styles in the middle of your ebook (or lack of any consistent style at all) will confuse people! And by the way, confused people return ebooks and ask for their money back!.
- Consistent formatting keeps people focused on the information in your ebook – not on your delivery process.

Number 5 – Keep "cute" clip art to a minimum.

- Don't use the clip art that comes with Microsoft Word, Microsoft Works or Microsoft publisher in your ebook! Two reasons for doing this:
  - **Number 1** – Microsoft forbids you to sell their clip art as part of a commercial work, and...
  - **Number 2** – people will recognize the pictures as Microsoft clip art that everybody uses and it will "cheapen" your work.
- Plenty of royalty free clip art exists on the Internet that not everybody uses. Make sure you put in a little extra effort into finding your clip art – if you choose to use it at all.
- We personally don't like to use much, if any clip art. If we ever did choose to include it we would use it very sparingly and only if it adds to the publication significantly.
- Don't fall into the trap of using pictures of meaningless clip art to make up for the fact that your book lacks valuable content.

Number 6 – Keep it simple.

- Don't get fancy in formatting your document! People want to read

the information and get what they wish for from your ebook – don't make them work to get through it.

- Don't get caught in the trap of using a bunch of different fonts because they looked "pretty" or "cool".
- Keep your text fonts, type styles and page organization clean and simple to read.

• Make sure that you include a complete table of contents that allows people to easily search for the information they need.

- Ebooks make it very easy to create links within your publication, so people can reference what they want without digging through the entire ebook to find it.

Number 7 – Use headers & footers for a cleaner, more organized look.

• You should put a copyright notice at the bottom of every single page of your document. Most word processors allow you to do this using the "header and footer" function.

• In most cases, the name of the book or the name of the publication along with your website and e-mail should appear at the top or at the bottom of every page.

How to Make Money with your eBook

When it comes to discussing the various ways you can promote your ebook online you'll find entire ebooks written about each one of these topics!

We will hit the highlights for you and give you direction on how to find out more information on each marketing and promotion method.

This text wants to teach you how to write your own ebook in seven days and publish it, but we also want to give you an overview of how to go about selling it when you're finished.

Please understand, however, unless we wanted to make this book a thousand pages long -we can only give you a good sense of direction and tell you where to go next.

What's in a Name? – Plenty!

Remember we talked about the importance of understanding the key words people will use to search for your ebook?

We told you that people perform searches using keywords in many of the online databases and bookstores. If you recall you did some investigation of

these sites to discover how they listed books when people entered key words looking for books matching their interests.

This means the key words you use in the title of your book, along with any description allowed, will really determine whether or not you show up in the search results.

Make sure that your title and description contain as many of the keywords people search for as possible – without going overboard.

For example: the name of this ebook "How to Write and Publish Your Own eBook in as little as Seven Days" contains three main keywords, "publish", "ebook", and "write".

Look at the key word results we got when I used the keyword suggestion tool for the word "ebook" at the search engine Overture.

You can look up keyword popularity at Overture by clicking here now.

(If that link ever goes down just email us and we'll let you know if it moved or how you can get access to it.)

The number to the left of each keyword phrase represents how many times someone searched for that word or phrase on Overture last month…

66735 ebook
13974 free ebook
1680 ebook reader
1299 free ebook download
1215 palm ebook
1172 ebook free
1143 ebook download
966 ebook software
858 rocket ebook
792 ebook publisher

See how our title comes up a little shy on most popular keyword terms?

To make up for that we must cram in the most popular keywords wherever we can offer a description of the book.

We would try to use this description (or something similar) wherever possible when listing our ebook in an on-line bookstore or giving away the first chapter at a download site.

"How to write and publish your own outrageously profitable **ebook** in only seven days-even if you can't write, can't type and failed high school English class! Sell or give away **free ebook downloads** to **ebook readers** all over the world and watch sales take off like a **rocket** as you become your own **ebook publisher**. "

See how many of the key words appear in this one?

Believe me – I understand the very fine balancing act you must play in naming your book and using keywords. We just want you to bear in mind that your choice of title and how you write your descriptions on various sites will directly impact on your sales!

I'm sure we'll play with this description a whole lot before we settle on one, while marketing this title in various ways across the web.

Get Yourself a "Killer" Two Page Website!

You can make sales without a website. Many people do this just by marketing through online bookstores. In fact, in the Bonus interview with Jay Conrad Levinson at the end of the book, we go over a number of different ways to get exposure for your book without owning a website.

However, if you want to break into big sales, sooner or later you must get a "killer" two page, sales letter style, website that sells your book like crazy!

Everything else we talk about from this point on involves either putting your book in front of people, actively searching for your subject matter at download sites and online bookstores, or using various marketing and promotion techniques to drive traffic to a website that sells your ebook.

So the first thing you must do – or darn close to the first thing – get yourself a website that you can use to sell your ebook.

Now before you start panicking saying "I thought this ebook would show me how to publish my ebook.", correct!

This book *shows* you how to publish your ebook – and once you publish it for distribution you then learn how to promote it… the same way a traditional author promotes his or her book once it gets published.

Good news! The definition of "website" changed significantly over the last few years. In the "old days" you needed a 30 to 40 page web site in order to look "legitimate" in the eyes of the online public.

In today's complicated and crowded online world the websites that really sell books like crazy contain only two pages –a sales letter and an order form where buyers give you their credit card and contact information. To make things even easier, if you use a service like **ClickBank**, you really only need a one page web site!

Here we explain how to create an effective one page sales letter for your web site.

If you follow these instructions you can create a killer web site that will sell your book better than anything else you could try!

As we already said, you can find people with entire ebooks devoted to the subject of creating one page sales letters and using them as a website.

One particular gentleman, Marlon Sanders, has an excellent program we recommend highly. Jim personally used the techniques in Marlon's program to increase sales on one of his websites by over 400% in only one week.

You heard me right!

Jim absorbed Marlon's information and took his existing 30 page web site and converted it into a one page sales letter with an order form. Jim got the exact same amount of traffic he generated all along and sales went up four fold!

Only the letter changed… Incredible!

By the way, this increase in sales helped make it possible for Jim to move into his new house!

So we would highly encourage you to **checkout Marlon's information (http://www.amazingformula.com/?167865)** if you want to get VERY proficient at creating one page sales letters that sell products like crazy!

Also, here we include about a dozen links to various one page websites that sell products like mad!

From these proven winners you will learn a lot just by reading them and looking at their common strengths and advantages.

As you read each sales letter, ask yourself:

- How do they use headlines and sub headlines?
- How do they format text?
- How do they format the web page?
- How do they use testimonials and endorsements?
- How do they draw the reader in emotionally?
- How do they express the reader's needs?
- How do they convince the reader to buy?
- What types of bonuses do they offer?
- How does their price compare with the value received?
- Does the message grab you and pull you in?
- How do they "close" you and get you to make the buying decision?

Look for the patterns they follow so you can create an absolutely outstanding one page website to sell your ebook

1. "Instant Sales Letters" (http://www.instantsalesletters.com)
2. "The Amazing Formula" (http://www.amazingformula.com)

3. "Instant Internet Profits" (http://instantinternetprofits.com)
4. "Gimme My Money Now!" (http://www.gimmesecrets.com)
5. "Ultimate Beginners Guide" (http://www.websitetricks.com)
6. "Guaranteed Marketing" (http://www.guaranteedmarketing.com)
7. "Turn Words Into Traffic" (http://www.turnwordsintotraffic.com)
8. "Internet Success Blueprint" (http://scamfreezone.com/bizop)
9. "Internet Success Diamonds" (http://scamfreezone.com/diamonds)
10. "Killer Copy Tactics" (http://www.killercopytactics.com)

First you must hook them with a compelling headline.

You get between three and eight seconds to grab a surfer's attention when they show up at your Web site. The headline will communicate the primary benefit they receive by reading the rest of your sales letter and, hopefully, buying your product.

A great headline, in case study after case study, increases sales by as much as 2, 3, 4, even 10 times over another headline!

Sit down and write out 10, 20 even 30 different headlines and see which one jumps out at you the most.

Next – write a letter.

Explain to people all the great stuff they'll get by purchasing your ebook.

Keep everything focused on their wants and needs and how your information will help them get what they want.

Use lots of bullets and sub-headlines and make sure to write short, simple and concise words.

No need to prove that you own a thesaurus and know how to use it!

Throw in a dash of "testimonials".

Now how do you get testimonials without selling any ebooks yet?

Simple! Get your friends who edited the book to give a testimonial with statements like "I used the techniques found in this book to get these **[specific]** results."

Now they don't say they use *your* ebook – they only say they used the *techniques* in your ebook, a fine line – but perfectly OK.

Careful though because anything more than that would push the line.

Never, never make up or fabricate testimonials because the law considers that fraud!

If your friends can't give you testimonials, or if you can only get one or two testimonials, then get some "display quotes" from some famous people.

You see them all the time… quotes from well known figures in society that endorse some course of action or pattern of thought.

Find yourself a good book of famous quotes and find a few that would support your ebook and inspire people to want to buy it.

If we wanted to motivate someone to write an ebook and let go of their doubts about their ability, I might use this quote:

> **"What the mind of man can conceive and believe, it can achieve."**
>
> — Napoleon Hill

These types of awesome quotes elevate your work to the level of the person you quote – an excellent psychological trigger.

Though this display quote technique doesn't replace an excellent testimonial, it can serve as a credibility builder until you collect testimonials from people who have read and benefited from your ebook.

By the way, you should constantly ask the people who buy your ebook to give you a testimonial once they use it.

Make sure those testimonials stay specific and emphasize the positive results they got.

For example:

"I used Jim's book and saved $6,810 in real estate commission by selling my house myself without an agent in only 2 1/2 weeks" sounds much better than "I read Jim's book and it was really good and I thought he was a great writer."

See the difference?

Someone halfway serious about selling their house will see that results oriented testimonial and say to themselves "*Hey, I'd like to get that result for myself! I'll buy that book.*"

Pile on the Goodies!

Next you want to make sure you use what my friend Yanik Silver terms the "bonus pile on."

Here you start sweetening the pot by throwing in extras for people, to the point where they feel like an absolute fool for not purchasing your ebook.

You can use bonus reports, other ebooks, and software... whatever your niche market wants!

Think about how we induced you to buy this book with the extra marketing information, free reports and more! We piled it on thick so you couldn't say no!

You can either write the bonuses yourself or you can find a number of free resources on the web.

** Often a collection of website addresses with valuable content organized around a central topic makes a nice bonus.

Side note: One of the most popular bonuses on Jim's real estate book site lists 7 sites that allow sellers to list their house online for free. Many sites charge $25-$50 per month for the same services we show people how to get for free. Saving just one month's charge on those sites more than covers the cost of the entire book!

See the value now of a bonus – or several bonuses – for buying your ebook?

You can even take some of the information you chose not to include in your ebook and expand that information into a related report. Length doesn't matter, only a highly perceived value in the minds of your customers.

Software that will help someone avoid effort or automate a tedious or time consuming process always makes an excellent free bonus.

… or your money back!

Next your sales letter should give a strong guarantee of the benefits people will receive by purchasing your ebook.

This usually means giving a 30, 60, 90, a 1 year or even a "lifetime" guarantee on the product. A strong guarantee increases sales since people feel confident that, if the ebook doesn't perform as promised, they can still evaluate it and get their money back.

Don't panic – write a good ebook and "over deliver" on the value and you shouldn't get more than a 5-10% return rate. Anyway, the increased sales as a result of the guarantee will MORE than offset any returns.

Take them by the hand!

You want to drive people to action! After you tell them all the great things they'll get, **tell them to click here and order now**!

Never leave them hanging, wondering what to do next!

P.S. – One last thing…

Finally you want to instill a strong sense of urgency in them and you do this best with a price comparison. If you build the value well in your sales letter then you can tell people what you sold the book for in the past

or, as a new product, what you plan to sell it for in the future! Let them see what a great deal they get by **acting NOW!**

Tell them you only guarantee to hold the price for a short period of time, such as 24 hours or three days. If they think the ebook will stay available at this price forever, they may not act as quickly as you would like.

You probably noticed, visiting the sites we listed above, that the majority of sales letter websites display a P.S. that says something to the effect that "We'll only guarantee to hold this price for the next 24 hours" or "We'll only guarantee you'll receive these bonuses if you order by midnight tonight".

"I could change my mind anytime so order now with it fresh on your mind!"

The authors of these letters usually say this in closing. They end their letters this way because it works!

So this basic structure for a one page website will work well in selling a single product – in this case your ebook. If you plan on achieving any level of success in marketing your ebook then it you must create an effective sales letter – ASAP.

The rest of the techniques we'll talk about next depend on achieving what many online marketers refer to as "proven copy" – which means how many ebooks does your website sell for every hundred people who show up.

Knowing that number along with your "proven copy," will let you really maximize the traffic generation strategies we want to discuss next.

Buy your way into the "Top 10" on the Search Engines

Would you like your website to achieve a "Top 10" placement on a major search engine? Who wouldn't!

Would you like it up there tomorrow, drawing tons of targeted traffic to your website like a stampede of cattle on the open Texas range? No problem!

Pay-per-click search engines offer anyone with a website the opportunity to obtain and keep a top spot in the search engines – no programming required.

Unlike traditional search engines, which base their selections on the page's content and "code", pay-per-click search engines sell their top spots to the highest bidder. When visitors search for a particular keyword phrase, the website owners who bid the highest come up first and get the lion's share of website traffic.

Getting to the top of traditional search engines can take months of effort and does not guarantee a good ranking, no matter how much effort gets expended.

Using the pay-per-click model short-cuts this extremely time and labor intensive process.

Overture.com, the web's top pay-per-click search engine, boasts millions of searches daily. Overture has been around for years, but recently started coming on strong with the decline in soft advertising dollars on the web.

In the past, traditional search engines made their money from selling banner ads and sponsorships to advertisers. Unfortunately for traditional search engines, advertisers finally learned that banner ads, general audience pop-ups, and other mass market, untargeted advertising techniques online, don't produce good returns on investment.

As a result, this formerly lucrative method of making money virtually disappeared for the top search engines – and Overture stepped in to fill the void.

Overture's search listings now appear in the search results of some of the web's traditional search engine giants, including:

- AOL
- Lycos
- HotBot
- Netscape
- DogPile
- Cnet and more!

For you as an advertiser, using Overture, or any pay-per-click search engine, is simple.

You sign up for an account on their site and pick out which keywords you think will bring you the visitors with the highest likelihood of buying from you.

You then "bid" to come up in the search results whenever a surfer performs a search for that particular keyword phrase. The higher you bid – the higher you come up in the results.

Studies have shown that the top three results in a keyword search get clicked far more than those appearing further down the results list.

If you ever want to come up higher in the search results than the site above you, just bid a penny more than they do and you will appear above them… until they bid higher!

Anyone who bids their site into the top few spots for a particular keyword phrase (Overture's "Premium Listings") not only appears in Overture, but also appears prominently on the first page of searches on those other search engines.

Overture in turn pays these search engines a commission for any of their links that get clicked by surfers. These arrangements finally evolved into a significant revenue source for these other search engines and massively extended Overture's reach across the Internet.

Overture's recent success launched a virtual online gold rush to cash in on the pay-per-click search engine model. Dozens of pay-per-click search engines have started up across the web trying to grab a piece of the pie.

FindWhat.com, the next largest pay-per-click search engine, dwarfs in comparison to Overture's size and reach. However, a recent price increase by Overture caused many of its lower volume advertisers to seek alternative pay-per-click traffic and FindWhat gladly welcomed them into the fold.

Anyone with a website who wants to get a jumpstart on traffic and start driving targeted visitors across their site, would do well to take a serious look at pay-per-click search engines. As the web gets more crowded, paying for search engine traffic represents an excellent way to rise above the clutter – fast!

The list of some of the TOP pay-per-click search engines online includes:

www.Overture.com

www.Google.com

www.findwhat.com

www.7search.com

www.Xuppa.com

www.goclick.com

www.Kanoodle.com

Get The First One FREE...

One of the more effective ways to get people interested in your book – give away the first chapter on your site and various download sites.

Now hear me out on this. This technique differs from giving away your book. Somebody started the idea that giving away an ebook would make a lot of money by using it to get people to come to your site.

Before the Internet got so crowded with various ebooks and little publications that people call ebooks –really nothing more than little, low-value pamphlets – this worked well for getting traffic to your site.

However, in this day and age, giving away an ebook will not, in most cases, work as an effective marketing tool.

Why?

Because "free" equals what you paid for it – nothing!

Nobody values anything they get for free as much as they value something where they paid a lot of money. In the payment of the money they see the value of the ebook.

Get someone interested in your ebook quickly by letting them read the first chapter. You can distribute this free chapter through download sites, your own website, other people's websites, and any other opportunity you can find to post it.

You don't need to use this marketing strategy – consider it one of many techniques you can use to hook people to buy your book.

Sell the Rights...

To illustrate this point please refer to the bonus interview concerning Yanik Silver and his "Million Dollar E-mails" book.

If you build a huge "back-end" into your book you can make a fortune by selling your book at low cost and then cashing in on customizing the book for all the people who want to resell it. Also, you can make money any time someone buys one of the products featured in your ebook through your affiliate link.

Yanik recently started selling his latest ebook and made tens of thousands of dollars up front in book sales and customization fees and now gets commission checks each month from various sources through his affiliate links.

Even though other people sell his book and keep the money, he back-loaded that ebook with many different opportunities for his readers to get more information. Every time someone buys a product from one of the people he profiles, Yanik makes money. He gets paid every single month as a result of people reading the book and buying the different items he profiles!

It rates one of the most exciting case studies I have ever seen as far as the various tips, tricks and tactics he uses to turn an ebook into a cash-generating machine that extends far beyond his own reach!

Ezine Marketing

The next way to promote your ebook and get traffic to your one page sales letter website, uses ezines.

People receive these electronic magazines or newsletters through their email box.

These subscriber-based lists get published on a regular basis around a central theme. They sometimes go out daily, but more often weekly or at least every two weeks. These newsletters in email form carry a common interest topic. The people who subscribe to these ezines must – at least in theory – want to know something about that particular subject.

Many editors of the ezines constantly look for new articles and advertisers for their publications. Speaking from personal experience, I find it difficult to come up with a fresh new article every single week – week after week!

Since we know you can write an ebook, it makes sense that you can write an interesting article about your topic. At the end of that article you can add a "resource box" with your contact information, email and website address. It tells people to go visit your site for more information.

By publishing articles related to the subject of your ebook it establishes you as an expert. Write up a good article and if an ezine picks it up readers will come to your website already considering you "the" expert on the subject and look for you to provide them with additional information – like the information found in your ebook!.

Several ebooks written on the subject of ezine marketing tell how to use it to grow your business quickly and effectively.

For the complete novice to the ezine world, we highly recommend that you take a look this site ===> **"http://www.turnwordsintotraffic.com"**.

You'll find the author, Rick Bettenau, in one of our featured author profiles. His book stands as a classic for anyone who wants the "down and dirty" on marketing to ezines. Ezine promotion gives one of the most effective and fastest ways to market your ebook and get traffic to your site on a shoestring budget.

Notes about Ezine Marketing:

Number one – before you submit an article to an ezine, go to their website and check out past articles to make sure you will reach your target audience. Nothing destroys your credibility with an ezine editor faster than submitting irrelevant articles for their audience.

Number two – don't submit more than two articles a month to the same ezine unless that ezine editor invites you to do so.

Look over these resources for additional information about marketing to and through ezines.

http://www.ideamarketers.com/

www.writerswrite.com/epublishing/newslet.htm

http://www.ezinesearch.com/search-it/ezine/

http://ezine-universe.com/

Why Reinvent the Wheel...

The next and most effective technique (in my opinion) for selling large quantities of your ebook comes from joint ventures with other, established marketers.

Look at people out there who already sell to your target market and you'll see they are a lot further down the trail than you. They finished all the legwork and marketing to compile lists in size ranging from 1,000 to 100,000 names of people who gave permission for those marketers to send them information relevant to their interests.

We know people with targeted lists of over 100,000 and they spend all their time looking for new products and information to introduce to their lists. Every time they mail that list they make between $20,000 and $100,000 in sales and they constantly want new, quality products because they simply can't produce them all themselves.

However, these super successful marketers follow a few rules and stay very protective of their lists. They treat those lists as real life gold!

Use these guidelines for dealing with potential joint venture partners – one of the most challenging yet potentially rewarding activities you can engage, in once you get the following:

#1 – You must have "proven copy".

This means you know your "numbers." You know that for every hundred people who show up at your website at least 2% purchase. Some websites never do better than 1% conversion while others can go as high as 5% or more!

Any joint venture partner will want to know the conversion rate for your sales letter before they consider doing business with you.

#2 – What's in it for me?

Next they'll want to know how much you will pay them for mailing their list endorsing your product. Many joint venture partners will demand as much as 50%, 60%… even 70% or higher of the purchase price of your ebook.

Unless you work with a significant "back end" (which means you offer additional products already in the hopper to sell to people who come into your pipeline) you may want to wait to do these types of deals until you

get some leverage – for example your own list of people to offer doing a reciprocal mailing of your joint venture partner's product to your list.

#3 – Scratch my back!

The third thing a large joint venture partner wants to know – what can you do for them besides paying a commission.

Joint venture partners know when they mail their list endorsing your product they, in effect, send you their *best* customers.

What do I mean?

If they email 100,000 people and 500 of them buy your book, those 500 people show their motivation and interest in what you do and what you sell. Therefore, the joint venture partner feels they sent you their best customers and they will want something in return.

Often they want you to do a reciprocal mailing – a real problem if you haven't compiled a mailing list. Without your own mailing list you should come up with some creative solution to give them something of equal value in exchange for the mailing.

In reality, even though you pay them a commission, the big boys and girls on the Internet want more than just the commission, they want to expand their own list and solidify their business. So bring more to the table than just saying to the potential joint venture partner "Hey, I'm going to pay you a nice commission."

They know you'll pay a commission – but they will want more than that.

Now don't sweat it – you don't stay the little guy forever. Someday your list will let you leverage a lot of other people to expand your list and skyrocket your profits!

Look at this example of a very successful joint venture.

Jim authored a CD ROM that sold information in the form of an ebook with 39 videos and several multimedia slide shows. The CD sold through joint venture partners to their audience with a high likelihood of interest in the CD.

The individual deals we made with these various joint venture partners depended on the size of their list and their prominence in the marketplace. We gave them a large percentage of sales, but in turn our product got recommendations and endorsements by some of the biggest names in that industry.

In the space of five months we sold about $100,000 worth of product! We don't know of any other way we could sell so many CD's that fast without spending a lot of money up front on advertising!

When you get "proven copy" and you know your "numbers", you owe it to yourself and your family to go find people already selling to the audience you want to reach and make them a sweet deal to promote your ebook. Once they do, you can virtually just sit back and watch the sales roll in!

A Remote Control Sales Force

Right along behind joint venture partners comes an Affiliate Program.

An affiliate program should sound relatively familiar to you. It lets people automatically sign up at your website as a "joint venture partner" with you. You don't do anything to sign them up or track their sales – especially if you use a service like <u>ClickBank</u> that allows people to automatically sign up and sell your ebook with no personal interaction on your part.

<u>ClickBank</u> will even process all the credit card orders, issue the affiliate checks every two weeks and do virtually everything else for paying affiliates and tracking their sales.

A word of warning – **DO NOT** try to set up an affiliate program first!

Until you get proven copy with your business system working, you will only create needless headaches for yourself by trying to recruit, motivate and retain a network of affiliates which you can't use just yet.

Plus, if you actively and effectively use ezine advertising and joint venture marketing you will find affiliates seeking you out once you can start handling them. Some of your early customers will eventually turn into your affiliates. Just make sure you use an affiliate tracking system that automates the sign-up and payment process for you.

Beyond Amazon... Alternative e-bookstores flourish online

Ask anyone to name the number one Internet bookstore and invariably they will mention the online bookselling giant, Amazon.com. Amazon spent millions of dollars cultivating a brand awareness that helped it survive while other "dot com" giants died off like dinosaurs.

However, despite its size and the impressive number of books it carries, Amazon does not represent the only place to sell books online.

[We do not endorse them – they just point you in the right direction.]

www.Ebookmall.com offers one of the largest selections of ebooks available online. Whether just casually shopping for the latest offerings or searching for a specific title or author, the site is well organized and makes it easy to shop and find what you want.

www.1stbooks.com offers an exciting twist on ebook publishing, in that you have a choice of how you want the book delivered. You can choose ebook, paperback or hardcover to receive your ebook. Though the selection is still growing, this type of flexible, consumer driven book delivery system will surely thrive in the future.An effective way to market your ebook online comes through online bookstores. We included a list of online bookstores (see below) you can visit, use and find more tools and resources to promote your ebook.

We also tried to create as wide a selection as possible, however, ebook stores come, go and change their services online every single day! After exhausting this list just pull up to your nearest search engine and search for online bookstores.

You'll find a ton of them with more popping up all over the place!

www.cyberread.com

www.ebook-case.com

www.ebooksonthe.net

www.ebookad.com

Go over this Yahoo! category pretty carefully: http://dir.yahoo.com/Business_and_Economy/Shopping_and_Services/Books/Bookstores/Electronic_Books/

A few notes of caution when dealing with online bookstores and electronic "publishers".

(This list may seem similar to the one offered in the section on Print on Demand publishers, but if you intend to deal with online bookstores you should read it.)

1. Make sure you retain the rights to your ebook. Don't let a bookstore or "e-publisher" tie up your publishing rights so you can't list your book in as many places as you want to.

2. Make sure you understand exactly how much you make off the sales of the books, when you get paid, plus the minimum payouts and compare the royalties offered between various sites.

3. Read over any contracts thoroughly. Don't sign or agree to anything you don't understand or don't feel comfortable with completely. An attorney should review anything that looks odd or just move on to another one of the many sites.

4. Don't succumb to promises of marketing help and distribution. These ebook stores will list your book – and little more! You will make sales if they get enough traffic to their site and someone comes across your ebook and buys it.

5. If you must pay money to list your book, make sure you understand exactly what you do and don't get for the money you spend. Sometimes spending money doesn't mean you'll get better results. Remember – you want to make more money than you spend!

6. CAREFULLY EDIT YOUR BOOK! Rarely will you find an editor "safety net". Nobody will edit your book for you at these sites – so any typos, misquotes, failure to credit sources, etc. fall on you and will show up in the book.

Author Interviews – Modeling Success!

The fastest way to learn anything, use the experiences of others – taking the good and making it your own while leaving their mistakes behind.

The following authors very graciously gave us their time and input to help guide you down the path to success in writing, publishing and marketing your ebook.

Learn from them!

Study what they did!

Avoid the mistakes they made!

Take their success tips to heart because these people already passed where you stand right now. Some of them are a little far ahead of you while others look back urging you forward.

Go for it!

Featured Author – Yanik Silver

Yanik Silver is a "results-only" direct response copywriter and marketing consultant who specializes in creating powerful tools and resources for entrepreneurs to enhance their businesses.

Before learning about direct response marketing, Yanik pounded the pavement selling medical equipment starting at the tender age of 16 when he first received his driver's license.

And actually it was a customer who gave him his first taste of direct marketing and it literally turned on the lights and helped him discover what he wanted to do at a young age.

He is the author of several marketing and practice building books including "*Instant Internet Profits*", "*Surefire Sales Letter Secrets*", "*The Ultimate Sales Letter Toolbox" and "How to Cash in on More Cosmetic Patients*".

Yanik is the creator of the successful "**Instant Sales Letters**" (**http://www.instantsalesletters.com**), a website where practically any business owner can create compelling and effective sales letters using easy, fill-in-the-blank templates.

And now his newest project is called "**Instant Internet Profits**" (**http://www.instantinternetprofits.com**), which provides a blue print for Internet success that nearly anyone can follow using his simple strategies.

When away from the office Yanik enjoys playing Beach Volleyball, Ice Hockey, skiing and working on his terrible golf game.

Surefire Marketing, Inc
7731 Tuckerman Lane # 162, Potomac, MD 20854
Phone 301-770-0423 Fax 301-770-1096

7DayeBook – *How did you get the idea for your book(s)?*

Yanik – The way I got my idea for Million Dollar emails as a direct descendant of my "Autoresponder Magic" book. I got the idea for that from a guy by the name of Mike Kimball who wrote an offline book called "The Ultimate Collection of winning Sales Letters" that he was selling for $15… and he gave away the resale rights to the book along with it. The tricky thing in there was that all the sales letters, except for I think one of them, all led into products that he sold.

He owns all the resale rights to the products and then stuck them in this guide. It was a nice product in that you could learn quite a bit about sales letters, but ultimately the goal was to get people to buy the stuff in the book.

7DayeBook – *So the book was sold under the premise that it would teach you about sales letters but actually it served also as a catalogue for the products he is selling?*

Yanik – Exactly! So I saw that I could do the exact same thing online – in fact it would be better because there could be direct web links in the actual book itself. It would be nice and easy and we would just put in affiliate links.

He also would sell you the resale rights to all the products in the catalogue for $10,000 – which gave me the idea that we could customize the ebook and charge $199 which made a really nice up-sell from the $19 sales price.

I saw from our market research from the sales of the Autoresponder Magic book (the ebook Yanik wrote prior to Million Dollar Emails) that people wanted to see follow-up messages and successful emails. I contacted a whole bunch of successful marketers online and got them to send me their successful emails.

From there I just compiled the letters into ebook format and included affiliate links for all the products.

NOTE: At the end of the interview we have for you a VERY special treat!

Yanik has very graciously spilled his guts about how he orchestrated the entire Million Dollar Emails ebook. He will guide you step by step as he compiles the book, gets other people to pay him for the privilege of selling it and launches a viral ebook explosion that still earns him thousands of dollars every month – with no additional effort on his part!

You MUST read this case study after finishing up this interview with Yanik… you can't afford to miss it!

7DayeBook – *So basically you modeled what you saw someone else doing successfully and moved it online and made it even more successful because of the convenience of having web links in your document. Excellent!*

What did you learn from that project to make your latest book, Million Dollar Emails, even better?

Yanik – From Autoresponder Magic I learned not to put the affiliate links as visible in the ebook because the readers could bypass our links. In Million Dollar Emails we just made the words with the link embedded in them. For example it would say Instant Sales Letters – but you would have to click the words… it wouldn't have the .com part.

Also, on the first page of the book we collect emails by offering a free report on psychology. Since other people are selling the book we had to have a way to get people to voluntarily give us their emails so we can follow up.

We offer a VERY excellent free report, that the only way people can get it, is to buy the book from someone and then email us for the report.

7DayeBook – *It sounds to me that you are a huge proponent of "back-end" selling because you sell the reprint rights to your ebooks. How do you make money doing that?*

Yanik – I make money several different ways when I sell the reprint rights.

First, and most obvious I make money when I sell the book.

Then I make money from the affiliate links if somebody buys something.

Next I make money from the $199 customization fee when someone wants to have us put their affiliate links in the book.

On this Million Dollar Emails project we had dozens of customization orders in the first few days!

7DayeBook – *How did you launch the Million Dollar Emails book once it was done?*

Yanik – The way I got the ball rolling was to send out an announcement to my existing list, which I have been compiling for about the last 2 years. If I hadn't had a list I would have found someone with a list and negotiated a joint venture deal.

From that initial mailing I made a little over $11,000 just on book sales. That doesn't include any affiliate sales.

7DayeBook – *WOW! So including everything, you grossed almost $20,000 in just a matter of a few weeks! Any thoughts on how much you'll make over the months from all those affiliate links?*

Yanik – I have no idea. It varies. Some months are good and others are okay. It takes a while to make money because the book has to work its way through the market.

With Autoresponder Magic we didn't really make anything from affiliate sales initially, but then after a couple of months we got up to around $1,000 to $2,000 per month in affiliate commissions.

7DayeBook – *If you had it all to do over again – what would you do differently, if anything?*

Yanik – The one thing I would like to do next time is to make it so everyone has to register their book no matter who they buy it from. That way you can send them value added information in the future and start building that relationship with them.

Another thing I might consider doing is not to give people the free resale rights, but make them pay $19 per month to resell the book. Make it more of a licensing setup.

I would provide a killer sales letter and fulfill the product.

That's about all I would do differently.

I have to say that if you give away the resale rights, your ebook will absolutely take off, versus trying to market it yourself. If the book is good you won't even have a chance to sell it yourself before other people are shooting it out to their lists.

7DayeBook – *So you better have a really good backend then?*

Yanik – Yes. You better have that backend set up already because once you pull the switch there's no turning back. Our objective is not only to sell books but to sell the customization as well – so we have to be ready to do both before we breathe a word of the book's availability.

The way I try to look at it, is always to look at it from the standpoint of the ultimate customer. So with the people who buy the book I want them to get a great ebook and the people who buy the customization to really go after their lists and make money. I want everyone to get the complete package – no matter what they buy.

I charge $7,500 to do a sales letter plus a 4% royalty. When I sell the customized book to my customers I make sure they get that level of value in the sales letter that goes along with the ebook… that's a huge bonus for only a $19 purchase.

Again, you must have your strategy planned out ahead of time!

7DayeBook – *What advice would you give a new author to speed up the success process?*

Yanik – The one biggest piece of advice I would give is to stop being such a perfectionist!

Most people are so darned concerned about every tiny detail about their book or their sales letter – and they end up with paralysis and never launch!

Get the thing as far as you can, polish it up and then release it to the market. You can always change it or tweak it later.

Unless it is a viral type ebook like Million Dollar Emails, that you have to have it right the first time, you don't have to be perfect right out of the gate.

With Instant Sales Letters I started out at $29 with thirty letters and now we're up to $39 with 65 or so letters. You can always add onto it and adjust the price – the main objective up front is to see if the market gets into it, then make adjustments.

7DayeBook – *Besides not being a perfectionist what advice would you give a new author?*

Yanik – The best piece of advice is to spend more time on your sales copy than worrying too much about your book. Make sure your book is good solid value and I will assume that you have good material in there.

But once you have that, your focus needs to be on the sales process and the sales copy you use to sell. In many cases I will write the sales letter offer before I ever write the product.

Don't ever write a book and then ask yourself, "Great, the book is done. Now who am I going to sell it to?" That's a

sure way to fail and get yourself totally depressed over the outcome.

7DayeBook – *What else would you advise a new author?*

Yanik – Don't get hung up in the technical aspects of the web. I'm a perfect example. I have no clue how to put up a web page but I just go to people who know how to do it and pay them.

If you can't afford to hire someone then there are plenty of low-cost resources out there that can teach you and help you put up your own web pages.

7DayeBook – *What type of research would you recommend to someone who is just starting out before they launch or even write their ebook?*

Yanik – The number one research is to research the marketing. Learn how to market online before you try to sell your book. You have to pay the price for success and immerse yourself in understanding what marketing works online!

Don't waste your time on biz-opp type kits and free stuff – pay the experts to teach you exactly what to do and how to do it. Those experts include: Jonathan Mizel, Marlon Sanders, Ken McCarthy, Cory Rudl and a handful of others.

Before I got on the web that is exactly what I did… and I never suggest anyone do anything I haven't done.

The key to the whole thing is understanding the marketing process and how to get your ebooks sold!

7DayeBook – *What daily activities would you suggest a new author engage in, understanding that they don't have a lot of time?*

Yanik – You have to engage in activities that will bring the maximum payback for you – and those are your marketing activities. It is not about getting your website perfect or tweaking your book. These include:

- Sending out ezine articles
- Posting to discussion boards and forums
- If you have an affiliate program make sure your site sells first! Don't do an affiliate program until you know the site sells.
- Engage in promotion activities daily – look to let people know exactly what you have to offer in a way that adds value rather than resorting to spamming or other interruption marketing techniques.
- Contact people with big lists to try to set up joint ventures.

7DayeBook – *Stop right there. How would you contact someone with a big list if you don't have proven copy or a big list to trade mailings with someone? How do you approach a joint venture partner?*

Yanik – You have to get traffic across your site to prove the copy and make sure your site can sell the ebook.

Get some pay-per-click traffic first and see how it converts. Initially you might not be able to land a big fish and you have to work your way up by working with people who have smaller lists until you graduate to the point where a "super" affiliate or joint venture partner will work with you.

Also, be prepared to give 50% of the sale or more to your joint venture partner. That's what people expect – especially when there is no hard cost involved! We give our best affiliates a big chunk of the sale because it motivates them and it costs us nothing to deliver the product.

7DayeBook – *But once you get enough people on your own list shouldn't you start looking to do mailings on other people's products?*

Yanik – Absolutely! Once you have your list together you can be the one making the lion's share by sending out information on products to your own list. Promoting other people's products is now a huge part of the revenue we enjoy.

7DayeBook – *What would you say the ratio is of content to sales pitches in your follow up emails?*

Yanik – We try to do a lot of content up front with the first 3 or 4 emails with nothing but value-added content. After that we try to do about 2 content pieces for every piece we send that has a direct endorsement of our products or another person's product.

7DayeBook – *What would you say is your most successful means of marketing?*

Yanik – Marketing to your own email list. If you don't have an email list do all the things we've been talking about. Also, run some targeted ads in various ezines. The best type of ad to run is a solo ad – which means you are the only ad in the whole ezine. The next best ad is a sponsorship ad and the least effective type of ad is a classified ad.

But if you can be the author of the article in the ezine, you need to shoot for that! The article is the way to get the best results because it presents you as "the" expert.

7DayeBook – *How do you find time to write all these books with such a busy schedule?*

Yanik – These last two books I probably only wrote 40 pages worth of my own material since they are compilation products. This is a great way for anyone who is really strapped for time to compile a book – get other people to give you their content and you recombine it in a new, innovative way.

Just think about one of the biggest selling books of all time – "Chicken Soup for the Soul"! All he did was take a bunch of inspirational stories from other people and combine them into a book. It has been wildly popular and look at all the follow up books to that series. So compilation products are nothing new – you just have to find an innovative way to put them together.

For me all I did was get autoresponder sequences and winning emails from people I did, and didn't know, and then pull them all together to make a winning ebook.

7DayeBook – *I want to wrap this whole thing up by asking you this question – How much experience did you have on the web before you wrote your books?*

Yanik – Honestly I didn't know anything more than how to surf. I took an existing product I was selling offline and brought it online. I made a lot of mistakes there and learned the ropes. I basically made every mistake people could make – I just made them in a short period of time!

The biggest thing I learned was that a straight sales pitch, one page letter, works the best! This is how you sell online.

Concentrate on the marketing – don't get hung up on the technology. Believe in yourself and your ability and just go do it!

7DayeBook – *Thanks Yanik!*

Yanik – It has been my pleasure!

"Million Dollar Emails" Case Study

====================================

How a simple ebook (that I only wrote a few pages of) created a massive profit windfall of $15,561.49 in less than a week

By Yanik Silver

====================================

I want to share with you the story behind one the quickest, easiest and most profitable projects I just put together. For some time, I had been toying with idea of viral marketing but I never tried anything so I decided on experimenting a little.

I wanted to create a viral marketing machine that would continue to produce recurring revenue for me years into the future with minimal work.

My plan was quite simple...

1. I'd get the top Internet Pros and eCommerce companies to submit their best email messages.
2. I would add my affiliate links so I can make recurring revenue if people click on the links inside the ebook.
3. I sell it for an ultra-cheap, price (but not for free so it retains value).
4. I let other people resell it (making it viral).
5. I give people the opportunity to get it customized for themselves (money upfront – plus they become my 2nd tier affiliates).

Okay, so after I registered a domain name – I started to get my content together.

I contacted Internet marketers and companies via email. The hot button I used for them was added publicity plus potential additional sales of their product for zero work (they already had the email campaign done).

Once I got the content together I worked on the offer trying to add perceived value. Here's what I came up with:

- Ebook for $19 includes the winning campaigns (and results) from the top pros.
- Bonus #1 is you can resell the ebook and keep all the money while using our proven sales letter.
- Bonus #2 is a special section of the ebook that contains the "101 Best email subject lines" and a critical checklist before sending out emails.

How about that?

Not too bad.

Once that was crystallized, I started creating the sales letter to sell the ebook. This is critically important. Since I was also going to be giving people the rights to use the sales letters – I wanted to create a dynamite sales letter.

I spent about 2 days writing and polishing this letter.

Next, I went to one of my favorite ebook cover designers, Vaughan, at killercovers.com and had him create the ebook cover design, my web site banner logo, and a full sized copy of the cover for the PDF file.

While that was being designed I worked on the other sales letter that sold the "Gold license" for $199 (an upsell inside the ebook to get the ebook customized with your own affiliate links).

I was completely blown away, when the first day I released the ebook to my list, we had people buying the Gold license.

All in all, the whole process took less than a few weeks once I got submissions from the contributors. I simply compiled everything into an Adobe PDF document using Acrobat (I have the full version), put my affiliate links inside the ebook and we were ready to roll.

Then I was ready to promote!

I first announced the ebook to my customer list and the orders just kept rolling in. It was great. My wife loved checking the email and she heard the little "ping" that meant another order came in.

Next, I went to my opt-in list and the sales just went through the roof! After all the dust settled I sold over 400 copies in just a few days. Plus, we still get orders every day for the ebook.

Remember the $15,561.49 figure I told you about in the title of this article? Well, that was just the first money I saw from the project. As intended, now I'm starting to see the affiliate commissions roll in.

Please understand I'm not trying to brag. I only bring up all these numbers to show you how easy it can be when you follow a proven system and model.

So what can you learn from this example?

A couple things...

First, it's better to sell tools. I imply that people are getting tools because they can model and "copy" the best email messages inside this ebook. And for the people looking to make money selling the ebook – I give them tools to sell it (the proven sales letter).

Next, the fact that you should think a little outside the box and think about what everyone is looking for. The contributors want free publicity, I wanted content, the buyers wanted tools, etc. etc. There's always got to be a benefit you need to identify for everyone involved.

Next, I created a massive viral marketing explosion because I gave people good content for a low, low price and gave away the resell rights.

Hope this helps inspire you to get your moneymaking project together. Just remember, it's not as hard as you think, especially when you've got a good example to follow.

Featured Author – Kevin Donlin

VERY Important – Kevin used a technique he picked up from Joe to churn out a high quality ebook with less than 24 hours of total effort! And what's more – Kevin will tell you exactly how he did it in this interview!

We especially love this interview with Kevin because he is living proof that the techniques we teach you work… and they work like crazy!

Kevin has been marketing online before there was a Web — he first sold an ebook on Usenet in 1994. Since then, he's researched and tested every possible online marketing method.

From 1995 to 1997, he was Webmaster for FedEx.com. His boss was the visionary genius who built the FedEx Web site ... and he personally answered more than 11,000 emails in two languages from customers worldwide. You could say he was present at the birth of online marketing and e-commerce ...

Since 1999, he's shared his marketing methods with entrepreneurs like you via his Guaranteed Marketing site and its companion ebook, available for free download — just send a blank email to **free-book@getresponse.com**

The marketing methods in his free ebook and **new manual** are proven and cost-effective. They combine the best of the Fortune 500 and small business worlds. And you get only the most-profitable ideas.

Amazingly, Kevin keeps current by reading 27 ezines, 5 print magazines and 2 books on marketing every month.

Kevin's primary website is **Guaranteed Marketing (http://www.guaranteedmarketing.com/).**

Let's hear what Kevin says about turning out high quality and outrageously profitable ebooks with record speed!

7DayeBook – *How did you get your idea for your book(s)?*

Kevin – The first ebook I wrote was called "Guaranteed Marketing;" this was in the summer of 1998.

I wrote it to share the marketing principles that had worked for me in my first business, Guaranteed Résumés, a résumé service that took the Internet (and my local market) by storm shortly after I opened it in 1996.

Since then, I've written "Résumé and Cover Letter Secrets Revealed" and "Guaranteed Cover Letters" for my résumé service business.

For my marketing business, Guaranteed Marketing LLC, I've written "How to Double Your Sales in 20 Minutes a Day with Follow-up Marketing" and "8 Secrets of $100,000+ Home Businesses."

I get the ideas for these titles by listening to what customers ask me personally and to what people on the Internet post to the discussion forums I participate in.

I try to find needs and fill them. If it sounds simple, it is!

Also, I periodically take a hard look at what I'm doing to make money in my own businesses. If I'm doing things in a systematic way that I believe will benefit others, then I consider writing an ebook to share that system.

That's how I got the idea for writting "How to Double Your Sales in 20 Minutes a Day with Follow-up Marketing." I literally did double my sales in 20 minutes a day, quickly breaking the $100,000 barrier, using a combination of sequential autoresponders and contact management software; it's dead easy, but no small business owner I know uses those two tools together effectively.

7DayeBook – *What would you do differently if you did it over again?*

Kevin – I would worry less about getting traditional PR by faxing out press releases.

Instead, I would spend more time building relationships with non-competitors and then structuring endorsed e-mailings to their subscriber lists, in which they endorse my ebook for a slice of the sales.

The more experienced I get and the wider my network of relationships becomes, the more I love this tactic!

I've made hundreds of dollars in just a few hours thanks to endorsements from the likes of Allan Gardyne and Phil Wiley, to name two strategic partners.

7DayeBook – *If you had to do it all over again what would you do the same?*

Kevin – I would write the way I do now, which is to **first bang out a rough draft as quickly as possible and then revise later**.

Never try to write perfectly the first time ... or even the second time!

I freely admit that every single one of my ebooks goes out with at least one minor error in punctuation, format or

spelling. And I don't give a flip. Because my readers are kind enough to point out the minor glitches they see and I'm quick to correct them.

If there are enough major snafus in an ebook, people will ask for their money back in droves… but luckily that's never happened!

7DayeBook – *What advice would you give a new author to speed up the success process?*

Kevin – Write about what you know.

If that's not going to be profitable, write about what you want to know.

In either case, passion is critical to success. If you don't have a passion for what you write about, you will fail. Every time! Because you won't have the drive and determination to pay the full price for success.

Second, I would strongly urge writers to spend 15 minutes each day building their network of possible joint venture partners — people who can introduce your product to their customers.

This is the fastest route to success that I know, but don't confuse it with a shortcut. You can't just spam (send unsolicited email) 100 influential people with emails asking for their help and then wait for the checks to arrive.

You have to help potential JV partners first. This can be anything from a brief email that says: "Hey, I read your book/bought your gadget/whatever and just wanted to thank you for the help you've given me!"

Then, a bit later, you can contact them with a free copy of your ebook for their review; don't ask for an endorsement at this point, just give it to them with your compliments. If they write back and say they liked it, then I would offer them a 50% – or higher – slice of the sales if they'd be willing to introduce it to their customer lists.

You only need to succeed a couple of times with this tactic to really enjoy some fantastic results.

Third, I'm a big fan of sending out article excerpts from my ebooks to Web sites and ezine publishers who ask for them. If you include a brief resource box at the end of your article, it's almost always more effective than a classified ad, in my experience.

7DayeBook – *What type of research would you recommend to someone, who is just starting up a web business to better ensure success?*

Kevin – Before writing a SINGLE WORD, do research to answer these two questions:

Is there a market for what I'm selling?

Use the top search engines to find out. At www.Google.com, type in terms that describe what you plan to write and sell; if you can't find a good number of pages, there's no market for it. Do the same at www.Overture.com (a pay-per-click search engine); if nobody's bidding on your terms, again, you probably have no market.

Who is my competition?

Too many competitors and you'll have a hard time cracking the market. Too few and you'll have to spend too much time educating the market on why they should buy your book in the first place.

If you find plenty of competitors, but none doing exactly what you're doing – or as well as you're doing it – then go forward boldly.

7DayeBook – *What daily activities would you suggest a new author engage in to market their book – understanding that they don't have a lot of time?*

Kevin – I think the #1 thing you can do to market your book is to have a well-run affiliate program that helps your affiliates make money. This is something I gradually learned over time.

Sure, it's quick (though not cheap) to buy top search engine rankings and get traffic to your site. It's easy (though not fast) to post at all the forums online and get visitors in dribs and dribs to your site. But an affiliate program is hands-down my favorite way.

Look at it this way. If you spend 1 hour posting 3 answers to tricky questions on online forums, you might get some traffic to your sales page, but it evaporates quickly.

But if you spend 1 hour on the phone talking with your top 3 affiliates on new marketing ideas, or writing an excerpt for your affiliates to send to their ezine readers/Web site surfers, those are activities that have lasting value, with infinite upside potential!

FYI, the best resource I've ever read on affiliate marketing — and I think I've read them all — is Jimmy D. Brown's "Free Advertising System"

Click Here ===> to visit the FREE Advertising System site

If you have a job and other obligations, you have to get up every day and spend at least an hour researching your market, finding joint venture partners and looking for high quality affiliates.

This will give you the highest return for the time you invest! Once you have affiliates, make sure you devote time to building a relationship with your top affiliates to keep them motivated and "up" about selling your product.

Also, take every opportunity to post information on the web on forums and discussion boards to show your expertise and then follow up with your resource box that has a link to your website. If anything, this keeps your mind sharp and keeps you in your market and up to date with what is going on RIGHT NOW in the market.

7DayeBook – *Did you make mistakes that others could learn from?*

Kevin – I've published one ebook that I didn't research the market adequately beforehand. I made the classic mistake of writing an ebook that I wanted to write, as opposed to one that people wanted to read.

Also, I waited too long to get more involved with managing my affiliates. You really can't be hands-off with your affiliates and expect them to be motivated enough to go out and sell your product.

7DayeBook – *What tools do you prefer to deliver your books and why?*

I just write my ebooks in Microsoft Word and then use Adobe Acrobat to create the actual file, because I have total control over how the product will look.

The Adobe Reader is free to download for users who need it and works on PCs as well as Macs.

Some writers prefer HTML versions of ebooks or programs that self-execute and open on the viewer's screen, but in my

view, that's more hassle than it's worth, and the final product doesn't look as professional as an Acrobat file.

7DayeBook – *Physically how do you take money and why do you use that method?*

Kevin – I use ClickBank to sell almost all of my ebooks.

Their software is quick and easy to integrate with any Web page. Customers can buy, download and read my ebooks within two minutes. ClickBank sends me a nice check every two weeks for my sales, minus their commissions.

Best of all, their e-commerce system comes with an affiliate program built right in; that alone is worth using it for!

7DayeBook – *How much do you make from the book and how is your compensation divided?*

Kevin – My ebook prices range from $9.95 to $39.95. My affiliates get 35-50% of the sales price, ClickBank takes a small percentage and I get the rest.

7DayeBook – *What is your most successful means of marketing?*

Kevin – Three methods: affiliate marketing, affiliate marketing, affiliate marketing!

7DayeBook – *How do you recruit high quality affiliates?*

Kevin – It's only something I've been doing for the last year. But the more you spend on other sources of sales, you realize that affiliates are a great way to make sales and they only cost if they make a sale.

I use ClickBank to manage my affiliates. Basically I believe you have to provide a lot of tools and motivation to keep them interested in your affiliate program as opposed to the 20 others they've joined.

Also, I tell the affiliates they will get support from me, 1 on 1, with a value of $197. That's what I charge for the kind of marketing help I give freely to my affiliates, by the way, and it encourages them to contact me and begin a relationship.

I am eager to give them this help for free because I want them to make money. I'm going to do it anyway – but I never put a value on it. As soon as I did my signups really accelerated.

I also send out regular mailings and trying out some contests to also motivate the affiliates.

7DayeBook – *What is your least successful means of marketing?*

Kevin – PR hasn't worked extremely well for me.

My friend David Garfinkel says it may be because the media are not ready to treat ebooks with the same level of respect that they do paper books printed in New York.

From what I've seen, I agree. I've spent several hundred dollars faxing out news releases that I think weren't half bad, but the results were horrible.

7DayeBook – *How do you find time to write with such a busy schedule?*

Kevin – I make time.

I treat the hours of 6:00 to 9:00 each morning, before I'm open for business, as "strategic time." This is the time in

which I work on the projects that will benefit me over the long term; writing ebooks is just one of them.

This is also the time I use to identify potential joint venture partners, find and contact "super affiliates" to help market my ebooks, tweak my Web pages, write advertising copy, etc.

7DayeBook – *Do you believe in backend selling? If "yes" How do you use it to make money?*

Kevin – YES! Every single ebook I sell has a backend; customers get anywhere from 5 to 25(!) follow-up emails from me with additional offers on ebooks, affiliate links, etc.

They can opt out at any time. I use the GetResponse.com autoresponders to deliver my backend messages, and anywhere from 10-30% or so of customers, will send me additional revenue this way.

If you neglect the backend, you're leaving a ton of money on the table, so it's crucial to plan every ebook with the entire backend strategy in mind.

I never put out an ebook without a back end and nobody should either!

Plus, when you start sending out emails to people right after they buy, and then on a periodic basis, it cuts down on returns – since people know you are still out there and are a real person who can help them out if they need it.

I like to contact my customers about every 1 to 2 weeks with informational content and follow-ups with other product suggestions I think they will enjoy and benefit from, based on what they have bought in the past.

7DayeBook – *What web trends do you see in the future?*

Kevin – More people participating in online commerce means there's never been a better time to be selling ebooks. But the bar will be raised higher in terms of quality. And you'll face increased competition, so your ability to identify and target a specific niche with your ebook will spell the difference between success and failure.

People are becoming more impatient every day. They want information that's fast and easy to use ... or they want their money back. So you have to develop a writing style that's easy to read on a computer or print out, with specific steps people can take to improve their lives.

7DayeBook – *What caused you to start your Internet business?*

Kevin – I first read about this thing called the Internet in a bookstore in downtown Tokyo, where I worked, in 1994. I knew immediately that my future had to have something to do with it. Sounds strange, but it's true!

7DayeBook – *What was your background in the area in which you started your business?*

Kevin – I first sold an ebook on Usenet in 1994; it was called "How to Find a Job on the Internet."

From 1995 to 1997, I was Webmaster for FedEx.com. I personally answered more than 11,000 emails in two languages from customers worldwide. Luckily, my bosses encouraged me to study and experiment with new ways to satisfy customers online, so that's now a part of my business mindset. You can do a lot worse than getting your marketing training from FedEx!

Since 1999, I've shared my marketing methods with other entrepreneurs via the **Guaranteed Marketing** site.

7DayeBook – *What challenges did you face in starting your web business?*

Kevin – Like most of us, it was not having enough hours in the day. Having to work full-time at my prior employer while getting my sites off the ground in the evening.

7DayeBook – *What challenges are you facing now?*

Kevin – Still not enough hours in the day!

I'm always reviewing what I do with the 80/20 rule in mind, which states that 80% of your results will come from just 20% of your efforts.

I try to reduce those low-value, tactical things that can eat up 80% of my day if I'm not careful.

Examples of wasting time: surfing aimlessly on the Web, reading less-than-helpful ezines, printing and reading Web pages that I'll just forget tomorrow, etc.

I try to focus on the high-value, strategic activities that might not make a buck today, but that represent tremendous earning potential down the road. Things like building relationships with affiliate, joint-venture partners and customers, or making improvements in my Web site, or testing new advertising approaches.

7DayeBook – *Tell me what a typical day is like for you in continually marketing your book and completing new projects?*

Kevin – I spend the first 30 minutes of each day answering email and poring over ezines.

During the next 30 minutes, I may post on one or two forums where I participate.

After that, I'll jump on whatever projects are ongoing – there's always something. I might review my sales logs to see which affiliates are selling the most.

I use ROIbot to track all my key advertising efforts and Web site links, so I'll review that information to see where my sales are coming from and who is generating sales right now.

7DayeBook – What challenges have you had to overcome with yourself in order to succeed as an ebook author?

Kevin – Writing and then marketing what you write takes tremendous self-discipline.

If it were easy, we'd all be millionaire authors. My biggest challenge lies in making the hard choices today on how I spend my time.

There are writing projects I can take on every day that will pay $100-200 a pop, but once they're done, they're done.

I'm more interested in creating more sources of long-term residual income. Which means I have to spend time writing ebooks, developing affiliates and building relationships.

Those activities don't pay off instantly, so it can be hard to forego a nice quick payoff today while laying the foundation for a nicer, bigger payoff down the road. It takes self-discipline and courage to do that.

7DayeBook – *How did you use an idea you got from Joe to write an ebook* ***in only 24 hours of total effort?***

Kevin – I got an email from Joe Vitale explaining how he had become interested in presenting "tele-classes" over three and four week periods.

Joe charges quite a bit of money for his classes which people pay for willingly because they get 3-4 weeks of personalized instruction from Joe – the expert.

So that email from Joe prompted me to look at the ebooks I had already written, to see if I should turn one of them into a tele-class. Then, I employed another technique you and Joe teach people, which is to make sure there is a market for your ebook before you write anything.

I took my Guaranteed Marketing book and sent an email to test the market first. I sent out an email to the people on my list that basically said "You've read Guaranteed Marketing and I can teach a class to you based on it – it will be more in-depth and it will be one on one assistance from me and it will be called Advanced Guaranteed Marketing."

I did this using the sales letter (which is available at the end of this interview) and I got some people to sign up.

At that point I realized that if nobody signs on, I don't have to write the tele-course, because there is no interest – I saved time by testing the market.

But people did sign up so then I had to write the course. I told them they'd be getting lessons every Tuesday starting about 3 weeks from when I sent out that first email.

I then broke my current book into 4 sections and I spent about 3 hours per Saturday afternoon, for 4 Saturdays in a row. I invested about 12 hours to expand the current sections of the book along with "Homework" assignments to prompt people to put each lesson into action in their business.

It took me only about an hour to take those 4 sections and then combine them into ebook form. So really, it only took me about 14 hours total, to create the entire ebook based on some existing content I had just created for the tele-class.

7DayeBook – *Do you feel like the fact that you obligated yourself to other people, set yourself up to HAVE to do the ebook, helped you get it done faster? Did you "burn all your bridges" so to speak so you would get it done, instead of doing what most people do which is to just sit around and hope and wish their ebook would get finished?*

Kevin – Absolutely! The deadline was a big part of it! I was forced to deliver because I was charging $497 to teach each of them the class.

7DayeBook – *But you also had a major reward waiting for you once the book was done – you got to keep the money!*

Kevin – You bet! Plus, in the process of delivering the class I knew I could repackage the information as a killer ebook!

Plus, I know I can turn this into a telephone-based seminar too!

I could also do an in-person seminar with it. So by looking at your project this way, it motivates you to create high quality content up front, so you can really make money with it several different ways without reinventing the wheel every single time.

7DayeBook – *As a BONUS – here is the letter Kevin sent out to his user base to get people to sign up for his tele-class. Could you use this technique with your own list or the list of a joint venture partner to make some immediate cash, as well as write the content for a fresh, new and "in-demand" ebook in record time?*

====================================

Announcing — Guaranteed Marketing Academy!

Due to the astonishing success of my ebook on small business marketing skills, I've decided to teach the first-ever course on "Guaranteed Marketing." And you're invited!

First ... you're receiving this as a follow-up to the "Guaranteed Marketing" ebook you requested from me. If you don't want to receive further messages, please see the unsubscribe instructions at the end of this message. Otherwise, feel free to forward the following to your friends. Thanks! — Kevin Donlin

OK. Here's what you'll get ...

Starting May 1, 2001, I'll send out four special e-mail lessons, one per week for four weeks, on four marketing topics. They are:

- Week #1: How to Create Customers for Life with a Powerful Guarantee that attracts buyers to your business like flies to honey. Your quality will increase, customers will love you, you'll leapfrog the competition, create powerful word-of-mouth advertising ... and that's just the FIRST lesson!
- Week #2: Your USP — Why You? Every business must have one to succeed. Does yours? Learn why "me too" marketing will kill your business. Your USP can strike fear into the hearts of competitors while driving throngs of customers to your door. But only if you do it right. This lesson will show you how, using the "Rosser Reaves" method to stand out from 80% of other businesses!
- Week #3: Four Ways to Grow Your Business. Make a quantum leap in profits by learning how to get more customers, who spend more and buy more often, all while reducing your

expenses. Benjamin Franklin said words to this effect — you can get rich by making more money or saving more money, but the fastest way is to do both at the same time. This lesson will show you how!

- Week #4: How to Create Referral Systems that turn your customers into a 24-hour sales force! Fact: customers who are referred to you will spend more and are easier to sell than any other group. Yet, how many small businesses have a system in place to generate referrals automatically? You'll come up with at least three easy ways to generate more referrals and explode your profits during this lesson — guaranteed!

Each lesson will expand on a money-making principle from my ebook "Guaranteed Marketing," which has received high praise from marketing legends like Larry Chase, Raleigh Pinskey and David Garfinkel, while being read by nearly 10,000 small business owners just like you.

Why is this course important for you? What can you do with this new knowledge?

Quite simply, this course is guaranteed to help you outmaneuver, outmarket and outsell your competition like never before. You'll recession-proof your small business, sleep better at night and enjoy new-found profits for years to come. Or your money back. (More on that guarantee later.)

Each lesson comes with my personal assistance, to help you apply the Guaranteed Marketing principles to your small business. There's no empty theory here! (Also, I'm a former English teacher, so I really CAN teach you.)

With my hands-on tutoring, you'll get the following assignments:

- write a blockbuster guarantee in week one,

- build a powerful USP in week two,
- discover four money-making ways to grow your business in week three, and
- create at least three automatic referral systems in week four.

After each lesson, you'll get my expert feedback and coaching on each of these marketing secrets. You'll quickly master this knowledge ... and profit from it forever!

Tuition for the four-week Guaranteed Marketing Academy, including my all-new curriculum and personal tutoring, is only $797. But sign up by Monday, April 16, 2001 and you can register for only $497 — you save $300! I accept credit cards, checks and money orders.

Since I give personal instruction to every student, the number of people in the course must be limited to just 10. So if you want to be one of the chosen few who laugh at recession worries, let me know right now! This one-of-a-kind course will never be repeated.

Is the course guaranteed? Yes! Sign up now. If you're not happy after the first lesson, tell me and I'll promptly refund your money. Every penny. You risk nothing!

Reserve your place in the new Guaranteed Marketing Academy by sending an email to me at gma@guaranteedmarketing.com. I urge you to do this NOW, as space is strictly limited to 10 people. Once those seats are gone, they're gone!

Here's what you'll get —

- You'll recession-proof your small business with marketing tactics, like an ironclad guarantee and powerful USP, that baffle your competition!

- You'll sleep better at night knowing your customers are out there, generating new business for you, 24 hours a day. Amazing!
- You'll find greater independence as you master not one but FOUR ways to grow your revenues! Your competitors will eat your dust after this.
- You'll enjoy unlimited wealth for years to come by turning your small business into a profit-producing laboratory that can't be duplicated by anyone else!

Or your money back.

Note: The Guaranteed Marketing Academy will begin Tuesday, May 1, 2001. You MUST register by April 16, 2001 to be included in this four-week business-building course. Remember, this is all done by e-mail, so you can receive and reply to each lesson at your convenience. I don't plan to offer this course again, so I urge you to sign up right NOW.

To register, send email to me at gma@guaranteedmarketing.com. Or, call me toll-free in the USA at 877-702-3487.

Warmly,

Kevin Donlin, Marketing Author

Click Here ===> http://www.guaranteedmarketing.com

Featured Author – Neil Shearing

Neil Shearing started out like the rest of us – he got really excited about the possibilities he saw online and just dove headfirst into the Web.

Neil has published a highly successful ebook that teaches "real" people like you and me the steps to succeed with an online business.

Neil's work has been featured and endorsed by some of the top names in online marketing and business opportunities.

Neil offers some excellent insight on various marketing and other techniques for ebook authors of all skills, abilities and subjects.

7DayeBook – *How did you get your idea for your book(s)?*

Neil - My products have always been based around filling a need. Usually the need came from me! If I was in desperate need for something, then I guessed that a lot of other people would need it too.

I know that's not as scientific as Marlon Sanders' "test twelve products" that he suggests in his "Gimme" ebook... but it has really paid off for me!

Click here to visit Marlon's site ===>

"http://www.gimmesecrets.com"

My first ebook, "Blueprint," covers everything I found out about creating and selling info-products online. It helped me make money, so I thought others would find it useful too.

Click here to visit Neil's site ===>

"http://scamfreezone.com/bizop"

The second ebook, Diamonds, was a result of my deciding that there was an overdose of information on the Internet. The top three secrets from ten of the top Internet marketers could be written down in about 50 pages...making a short, powerful ebook.

I was excited to learn the secrets, so I expected the book to sell well!

Click here to visit Neil's site ===>

"http://scamfreezone.com/diamonds"

My latest product, Internet Success Spider, is software that I just really wanted!

You know when you do a search for websites that link to you on AltaVista? Well, I just wanted those links to be in some sort of order... so I had a programmer write a script that puts the links in descending order based on how "popular" a site is (the number of links into it). Then I realized that I could use the software on other sites, find out their biggest and best link partners and approach them for a joint venture or reciprocal link!

The software has sold like crazy because it *filled a need*.

Click here to visit Neil's site ===>

"http://scamfreezone.com/spider"

7DayeBook – *What would you do differently if you did it over again?*

Neil – Phew. That's a big question!

I guess I would have taken a more "gung ho" attitude. I built up my online business very slowly, as a part time venture, while I finished my PhD.

I've been online since 1997, but have really only been strongly pushing the business this year, and I've quadrupled my sales since taking the bull by the horns!

7DayeBook – *If you had to do it all over again what would you do the same?*

Neil – I would put the customer first, second and last!

Publishing ebooks is not about you, me or the technology… it's about meeting the needs of the customer and helping them get what they want.

If you constantly look at your business from their point of view, including everything from how fast your page loads, to how you respond to emails for more information, you will see what needs to be improved.

I'm constantly searching for better ways to help my future and existing customers.

If you put the customer at the center of your business, you're almost guaranteed to succeed.

7DayeBook – *What advice would you give a new author to speed up the success process?*

Neil – As I already said, go "gung ho". Jump in there and get your feet wet.

Learn HTML and FTP… I don't know how many times I explain to people, they are drop dead simple.

(NOTE: HTML and FTP are making web pages and uploading them to the web. This operation has become VERY easy in the last couple of years due to highly simple yet powerful software, that makes it possible for anyone to make and upload a great web page.)

Don't be scared of getting your own domain name and web-space. Look at it this way...you're smart, right? You can tie your shoelaces...so get moving.

This stuff is not rocket-science; people just try to make it seem like rocket science, so that you'll buy their books!

Speaking of which, you have to be prepared to learn.

Nearly everyday I learn something new.

If you don't want to learn new things frequently, and adapt all the time, fine...flip burgers...but the way I see it, constant change is spelt "OPPORTUNITY"!

7DayeBook – *What type of research would you recommend to someone who is just starting up a web business do to better ensure success?*

Neil – During my time as a PhD student, I realized that I'd reached the cutting edge of knowledge. It was no longer sufficient to read text books, they were too far out of date, or too general.

So I read research papers, and attended conferences to get the latest up to the minute information.

It's the same with the Internet. This knowledge is all SO new, that you can't read a book from the local library and expect to have the latest knowledge.

You have to read the latest ebooks, from the top marketers, as soon as they appear.

One step better is to read newsletters – not the freebie ones, because they don't contain the cutting edge, valuable info.

I mean the ones you have to pay for because they're so valuable…an example is Stephen Mahaney's "Search Engine News".

Stephen once told me that his team works frantically the day before each release with new additions...now that's the info you want to be reading!

http://www.scamfree.com/sehelp/

7DayeBook – *What daily activities would you suggest a new author engage in to market their book – understanding that they don't have a lot of time?*

Neil – I would suggest posting questions and answers to forums.

You have to make some time to do this, but it gets your name exposure, and, if the forum allows you to post a link at the end of your message, you can put your website address...that will count towards the link popularity of your site and give you a boost in the search engines :-)

7DayeBook – *Did you make mistakes that others could learn from?*

Neil – I think most of my major mistakes were sins of omission. In retrospect, they look like mistakes, but at the time I wasn't aware how much money I was losing!

For example, before a customer orders, offer them an upsell... an improved version, an added extra, for a few dollars more.

Also, follow up with several personalized emails after the customer orders. This reassures them that you're still

there...and permits you to email them your next product when it's ready.

Finally, stay in contact with your customers. Don't let them wander away. Keep in contact and that customer will do business with you for life!

There's two ways to set this up. Either use the autoresponder system that I use at Get Response...

Click here to visit site ===>

"http://www.getresponse.com"

...or use the "whole shebang" system from Merchant's Choice...

Click here to visit site ===>

"http://www.1shoppingcart.com/"

7DayeBook – *What tools do you prefer to deliver your books and why?*

Neil – At last, an easy question!

I go over this in "Internet Success Blueprint". Basically, I think Adobe Acrobat is miles ahead of anything else.

—> You can create small documents for free at:

https://createpdf.adobe.com

—> You can password protect the file so there's no option to "copy and paste".

—> Acrobat Reader is a free download, and works on nearly any system...unlike most executable ebooks which need Windows and Internet Explorer.

—> PDF files cannot be infected with viruses, so they're better than offering Word documents or executable files.

7DayeBook – *Physically how do you take money and why do you use that method?*

Neil – I take credit cards on a pre-authorization system. That means I have to manually click a button to process each charge, which is a bit of a drag...but it serves two purposes.

Firstly, I screen fraud better than any script could...so I've cut charge-backs to virtually zero.

(NOTE: Charge-backs are when a buyer requests their credit card company get their money back. This is different from a refund since a charge-back usually results in not only giving back the buyer's money, but also paying a $20-$30 fee to the credit card company for getting involved. Charge-backs are bad and should be avoided at all costs through providing excellent customer service and responding the buyer problems quickly.)

Secondly, if my customer isn't happy with the product, they let me know within 48 hours and I don't charge their card. This gives me a unique selling position (I call it "the best digital guarantee ever"), AND, unlike processing a refund, if I never charge the card, I don't lose any processing fees.

To the customer, this is all hidden. They simply put their card though and download the product after authorization.

I also take checks and PayPal orders.

7DayeBook – *How much do you make from the book and how is your compensation divided up?*

Neil – I make 50% and my associates make 50% from each sale...that just sounds fair to me.

It's also one of the most generous programs you'll find online. Especially as I offer an additional 10% on sales

generated by referred associates... in which case I only make 40% ;-)

Click here to visit Neil's affiliate site ===>

"http://scamfreezone.com/assocs"

7DayeBook – *What is your most successful means of marketing?*

Neil – Definitely the search engines.

I think link popularity is very under-rated. If you have a lot of links...real ones, not from link farms or FFA pages...the search engines give you a huge boost.

I've maintained top positions in AltaVista for "home business" and "home business opportunities" (and sometimes "business opportunities") for literally years *without trying* by maximizing my link popularity.

My latest product, "The Spider" really helps with this technique because it identifies and "super links"...the sites that have a lot of links into *them* from any website you choose.

When they link to you, your search engine rankings can go through the roof!

Click here to visit Neil's site ===>

"http://scamfreezone.com/spider"

7DayeBook – *What is your least successful means of marketing?*

Neil – Sitting on my backside not doing anything.

Most marketing works if you put in some effort.

I guess FFA (free for all) pages are the worst in terms of results vs. spam (unsolicited email) received...but I think I only used one once. That was enough to put me off! :-)

(NOTE: FFA's – Free For All links pages –pages and pages of links to other sites. Initially started to increase link popularity, in many cases, they degenerated into nothing more than web sites that collect email addresses to spam people with unsolicited email.)

7DayeBook – *How do you find time to write with such a busy schedule?*

Neil – I simply love to write. :-)

When I think about it, I write webpages, articles, newsletters, emails, ebooks, and more!

I guess this isn't really a game to be in if you're not comfortable writing.

7DayeBook – *Do you believe in backend selling? If "yes" How do you use it to make money?*

Neil – Once you've developed your relationship with your customer by offering them great products, quality service, and bonuses that they love... you can briefly mention that someone has released a tool that you think is amazing and provide a quick link.

That's it. That's backend selling. And it's tremendously powerful. But you have to invest time in cultivating a relationship first.

7DayeBook – *What web trends do you see in the future?*

Neil – This isn't really my forte. I just react to holes in the market. I don't try to predict the future.

Having said that, I see the whole Internet bubble repeating itself when broadband (cable and DSL high speed connections) arrives for the masses.

I see the future as nothing but rosy when people get broadband access and can load pages in seconds instead of minutes. Get in now!

7DayeBook – *What caused you to start your Internet business?*

Neil – Hmm. I always had an entrepreneurial streak in me... I just didn't know where to use it. I didn't want to be in charge of a company with overheads, factories and staff.

As a result of the education system, I took Science as far as I could, but during my PhD in breast cancer research, I realized that I didn't enjoy the day-to-day benchwork.

At the same time I starting looking for something else, the Internet burst onto the scene. Instantly, I saw something that I would enjoy doing, and it gave me that entrepreneurial outlet for which I'd always been searching.

It really is magical when you can see someone from New Zealand buying your ebook overnight, downloading it and reading it. After a few days, the money appears in my bank account. What a business!

It's also great as a creative outlet...I've done all the graphical work on my sites except for the ebook covers.

7DayeBook – *What was your background in the area in which you started your business?*

Neil – Absolutely zip. I had no experience. Period.

7DayeBook – *What challenges did you face in starting your web business?*

Neil – The same challenges that everyone else has faced... the initial learning curve, the creation of a product, the writing of sales copy, the understanding that people online are not in a "buying" frame of mind and how to overcome that, the problems inherent in the banking system (who are dinosaurs) etc., etc.

7DayeBook – *What challenges are you facing now?*

Neil – I'm trying to automate as much as I can. I figure that if I do something more than twice a day, there should be a shortcut!

So I have software that types "Thanks for your email." when I press CTRL+T, and many, many more using nifty software called QuicKeys from...

http://www.cesoft.com/products/quickeys.html

Automation is a major goal because it frees up time to do or learn other useful actions.

7DayeBook – *Tell us what a typical day is like for you in continually marketing your book and completing new projects?*

Neil – That's a tough question to answer. I guess most of my marketing is done by email. I try to respond to emails instantly. Of course, that rarely happens, but I'm frequently complimented on the speed with which I respond.

I figure that people hope for a response within 2 hours, so if I get back to them more quickly, I've helped make that relationship just a little bit stronger.

Apart from that, I just do what comes along.

- I write to previous customers.
- I write my newsletter.
- I write to my associates.

- And I take any quality opportunity to participate in things like this interview!

Usually there's not much time left to do anything else!

7DayeBook – *How much experience did you have with the WWW before you started your business?*

Neil – Very little. I just jumped onto the Web and found a mechanism for selling a report without any upfront fees or monthly fees.

I thought that was amazing, so I sold the idea as a bigger report which has since morphed into the 279-page ebook called "Internet Success Blueprint".

Click here to visit Neil's site ===>

"http://scamfreezone.com/bizop"

7DayeBook – *What challenges have you had to overcome within yourself in order to succeed as an ebook author?*

Neil – I've had to change my style of writing. As a scientist, the prose is very, very dry. On the Web, the opposite works... punchy, quick, sharp, exciting is what people want!

Apart from that, I guess a major personality challenge was overcoming a lack of focus.

I tend to start a million projects and never finish any. I've been forced to make sure projects are completed before I move on.

It's also quite a challenge to work from home.

Most people say "Oh I'd love to work from home, it would be a breeze".

Yes, it is a fantastic way to work...but it can also be tricky when there's football on the TV, or my son is crying downstairs, or the coffee maker is begging you to take a break and have another cup of coffee....lots of distractions.

The trick is to love what you do...then the distractions fade away as you get excited by another day on the Internet...unlike any day before it :-)

Best Regards,

Neil Shearing

"Everything You Need To Know About Internet Success..."
"Internet Success Blueprint"

Featured Author – Rick Beneteau

In late 1996, Rick logged on to the Internet for the very first time. The challenge to conquer what he refers to as the "Wild, Wild Web" was too great to resist.

1998 found him one of the pioneers of the 2-Tier Affiliate Program, now so prominent on the Internet, with the highly touted and successful I.D. IT! Plates Partner Program.

He also began writing business articles in a style still not seen very often on the Internet. His friendly, wit-driven articles soon filled the pages of most of the prominent ezines and newsletters.

Rick's first ebook entitled "The Ezine Marketing Machine" was released October/99 and has since become an Internet-wide best-seller. Rick has just released another ebook, destined to remain another top-seller, "Branding YOU and Breaking the Bank".

The New Millennium finds the 46 year-old busy with the growing of his Internet company, Interniche.net , his "E-chievement" Ezine – The Mirror, his two powerful 2-Tier Affiliate Programs – EZineMoney and the I.D. IT! Plates Partner Program as well as the start up of 2 new affiliate programs.

Rick is a bundle of energy and, quite frankly, we had a hard time getting him to sit down long enough to do this interview – but we know you will enjoy his wit and insight.

7DayeBook – *How did you get your idea for your book(s)?*

Rick – Well, being a totally right-brained Virgo (yes, I'm cursedJ), the ideas come rather easily. In actuality, in my existing books, **The Ezine Marketing Machine** and **Branding YOU and Breaking the Bank** I teach by simply telling the stories of how I've come to enjoy the success I have.

These 2 books I HAD to write, because if I can achieve this level of success – anyone can!

7DayeBook – *What would you do differently if you did it over again?*

Rick – Not too much, and I really mean that.

Call it luck or plain common sense, but how I approached the Internet has really worked.

From the countless testimonials I've received, I know in my heart that my articles and my products have done a lot of people a lot of good and that's what matters most.

On the marketing side of things, as a pioneer of the 2-Tier affiliate system (I.D. IT! Plates was the first two level program, as far as I know), leveraging the power of over 15,000 resellers. It has proven to be extremely successful and I plan to market future products in this manner.

Further, I do my best to provide effective promotional resources for my partners, use what is by far the best affiliate tracking software for my people, and my customer support I can proudly state is second to none.

7DayeBook – *What advice would you give a new author to speed up the success process?*

Rick – I hope it goes without saying, that to create a product with the clear intention of benefiting your customer, is first and foremost.

Building strong strategic relationships with powerful people is of prime importance.

An example of that is this very interview. Had I not been known to Jim and Joe, well, you'd be reading someone else's interview here and not mine.

I teach this very thing in **Branding YOU and Breaking the Bank**. Being recognized as an "expert" in your field is absolutely key!

After that, I strongly encourage new authors to use the power of an affiliate marketing system to sell their book – and, implement a well-designed, affiliate-focused system, like mine.

7DayeBook – *What daily/weekly activities would you tell a new author to engage in religiously, to promote their book, if they have no money?*

Rick – It doesn't cost you a rusty nickel to get yourself well known on the Internet.

Again, Writing articles, posting (sensibly) in the myriad of web-boards, newsgroups and discussion lists (related to your area of expertise) on the Net, while building a "human", friendly and solidly informational website are among those steps. None of this is difficult to do!

7DayeBook – *What type of research would you recommend to someone who is just starting up a web business to better ensure success?*

Rick – I strongly encourage new Internet entrepreneurs to thoroughly study the websites (from ALL aspects) of 3 or 4 of the top marketers.

I mean spend quality time to learn what they offer their visitors (who will likely turn into customers at some point) and exactly how they present their wares to potential customers.

Specifically what you should look for on these sites:

- See how they "capture" subscribers
- Subscribe to and study their publications to see how they "relate" with their subscribers
- Study their sales letters
- BUY their products not only to learn how they benefit their customers but to see how their products are constructed and laid out.

The best teachers are those who are doing it right now!

7DayeBook – *Did you make mistakes that others could learn from?*

Rick – Yes, in my haste to complete some new projects, I allowed a most unfortunate situation to occur recently.

There's no better way for me to tell you about it, than to point you to an article I wrote, that describes in detail what happened:

http://www.interniche.net/article/congame.htm

NOTE: We debated long and hard about including this article in the interview, but ultimately decided you should be aware of potential for problems.

We want to stress however that this is a very small and infrequent exception to the rule! There are bad people out there – but they don't just operate online. Read Rick's article with the purpose of protecting yourself, but don't let it scare you from getting started.

7DayeBook – *What tools do you prefer to deliver your books and why?*

Rick – I use Ebook Edit Pro to compile my eBooks. Simple to use, and compatible with every PC operating system (which most other compilers are not).

You may want to offer Acrobat PDF files for Macintosh users.

To deliver my newsletter, The Mirror, and, affiliate program updates, I've installed MailMasterPro on my server. This program is automatic and easy to use all the way around.

As I mentioned before, I am a fanatic about the affiliate software I use because it resides on MY server and allows me, and my partners, a lot of flexibility that other systems do not.

Pricey, yes, but well worth it in the end. I'm a big believer in controlling my systems and my finances and therefore do not use 3rd party systems. That's not to say they won't work for you and give you a less expensive alternative to starting up.

I also use some cool tools for other purposes like TextPad (MS Notepad on steroids) for formatting my newsletters, Extractor Pro (old spam toolJ) for filtering removes and formatting email addresses, PerfectKeyboard (macro program) for instant pasting of templated responses (support issues) and I also use, gulp, Microsoft Front Page for webdesign as I'm html-challengedJ

Something else. When you grow to a certain size (you'll know when it's time) get your own dedicated server. But

make sure if it's co-located, you have a dynamite, support-oriented webhost like I do. Very critical!

7DayeBook – *Physically, how do you take money and why do you use that method?*

Rick – I believe in controlling my own systems and finances. I have my own merchant account with real-time processing incorporated into my ordering system.

This may be somewhat expensive for a new author to undertake. However, as mentioned before, there are third party systems available that take varying percentages for transacting your purchases and administrating your affiliate program.

7DayeBook – *How much do you make from the book and how is your compensation divided up?*

Rick – As to your first question, if I told you, I'd have to kill you!J

Both **The Ezine Marketing Machine** and **Branding YOU and Breaking the Bank** sell for $29.95 U.S.

My 2-Tier affiliate systems pays 30% on the first tier, and 20% on the second for all these products, with a modest commission minimum payout.

Partners are paid each month for the previous month's sales.

Suffice it to say, each book sells well. **The Ezine Marketing Machine**, despite its release in October 1999, is still a top-seller!

7DayeBook – *What is your most successful means of marketing?*

Rick – Again, it's the affiliate program. Nothing beats having 15,000+ resellers out there.

I don't promote my books directly other than by writing articles (where my resource box leads to the book's website), doing radio interviews and written interviews such as this and of course joint ventures with other marketers.

Of course, I "rollout" each new book to my existing partners, as well as place listings for each program in the many affiliate program directories on the Internet.

7DayeBook – *What is your least successful means of marketing?*

Rick – Funny, it's Friday the 13th as I answer Question 13, a "least" question.

Although I have very limited direct experience in such things, I know that FFA links, classified ad sites, spam email (this will kill your reputation and quickly too), banners and banner exchanges, and safelists, by and large don't work.

If you don't write articles (if you're an author I don't know why you wouldn't use this fast, FREE publicity vehicle), well-written ads in quality ezines do work. So does becoming recognized in major web-boards, newsgroups and discussion lists as a respected expert in your area of interest.

7DayeBook – *How do you find time to write with such a busy schedule?*

Rick – Simple. I make time. I'm far more creative in the first part of the day so I'll schedule a few hours in the morning in which I seclude myself to write.

No phones, faxes, email or ICQ's to interrupt me. Just me and my laptop on the backyard patio or on the front porch swing (where I am nowJ)

Writing is a passion but also a discipline. Even if I don't naturally "feel" like writing, the simple act of just doing it will usually spark the creative juices and make for a productive writing session.

7DayeBook – *Do you believe in backend selling? If "yes" How do you use it to make money?*

Rick – I'm referred to quite often as the antithesis of what Internet marketers should be.

When I discuss my sales and traffic with my friendly competitors, they are amazed, because I don't push back-end products very hard (I do point to a few useful tools in my books, some free and for some I'm a reseller. But I NEVER back-end a product that is necessary to have to implement the methods I state I will teach in the eBook they just purchased) and I don't use sequential auto-responders and the highly-touted new viral marketing techniques.

I've always relied on "Personal Branding" for my results. But I wouldn't suggest a new author dismiss such marketing tactics as they've proven too successful for countless marketers.

7DayeBook – *Are you working on any projects right now you'd like to give us a preview of?*

Rick – I'm glad you askedJ

I've been asked too many times over the past 2 years to make available a print of my "Entrepreneur's Prayer", which has appeared in countless business, marketing and self-growth ezines not to mention magazines and print books.

When I had finished writing the more recent "The Legacy You Leave" I had the feeling it would positively impact people on the same scale (and it has started to do just that) so I had no choice but to make prints of both of these available.

So, I retained a top graphic designer and now offer beautiful 11" X 14" laminated prints individually, or in a set, at very LOW prices.

You can check them out here:

http://www.rickbeneteau.com/

7DayeBook – *What web trends do you see in the future?*

Rick – I'm not a "trendy" kinda guyJ – but I believe we will be seeing a dramatic increase in paid-for content on the Internet.

Much like when HBO and the cable industry started charging for better programming, when television was totally free, as the Net is now.

That, and the Web becoming a much more "human" place. The latter, I wrote about in my very first article, The Unwritten Law of You, which really started it all for me 3 years ago.

Bottom line, the big "dot-bombs" coulda learned a whole lot from the little guysJ

7DayeBook – *What caused you to start your Internet business?*

Rick – Desperation. Literally!

I actually tell the entire story in **Branding YOU and Breaking the Bank**. I sold a very successful multi-store dry cleaning business in the 90's in order to start a music production company (I had enjoyed success as a part-time songwriter since the 80's – you can hear some

MP3's of my music here) but a nasty divorce claimed my newly-built studio and financial asset base for that costly endeavour.

When the dung hit the spinning blade, I was not only broke, but very deep in debt so I took a look at the Internet for the first time in late 1996 as a "possibility". I felt I could "somehow" make a go of it in cyberspace, as small as it was back then.

I've been building a list of quotes over the past year (for speaking engagements and future book purposes) and one of them is:

"Loss creates a vacuum into which something greater always flows."

One of the universal truths that was fully realized in my life!

7DayeBook – *What was your background in the area in which you started your business?*

Rick – As I've already mentioned that BI (Before Internet), I was a drycleaner, going into business right out of high school. Then, as a songwriter, I had my songs recorded by many artists and actually won the Billboard Magazine Songwriting Competition in its first 2 years.

I also had the privilege of writing and working with some of the world's greatest songwriters, artists, musicians and producers.

I believe I've utilized the business and creative skills I've been blessed to acquire in my life in everything I've done to date on the Internet. Further, I strongly believe that everyone has skills and talents that they can "bring to the cyber-party"!

It's only a matter putting their desire and determination into motion to make it work!

7DayeBook – *What challenges did you face in starting your web business?*

Rick – When I first logged on to the Internet I was as green as the money I needed to make. I simply put my abilities and my belief system to work for me, making a few strategic but short-lived mistakes along the way.

It is imperative to mention that there were no real e-teachers in 1996, whereas now there are several successful marketers whose expertise you can acquire very inexpensively, to help you "arrive" very quickly and surely.

Simply put, you can avoid most of the potential start-up challenges by learning from those of us who have invested their time, effort and money learning what, and what not, to do.

7DayeBook – *Tell us what a typical day is like for you in continually marketing your books and completing new projects?*

Rick – Well, as stated earlier, I don't "continually market" because I have over 15,000 resellers doing that for me, however, my typical day begins around 5 or 6 a.m. (I LOVE the morning) with this little sequence where I boot-up my computers, kick start the java machine (that would be coffee), get out the vitamins (I don't do brekkie) and start a list of the day's to-do's.

Once planted in my office chair, I open my email client which fires up my DSL modem and deal with the critical email ie: customer and reseller support, JV partner communications, request to reprint articles etc.

If I'm writing (book, salesletter, promos etc.), as morning is my "creative time", I'll carry my laptop outside and get to it. If not, I'll finish up my email and go on to returning/making phone calls, webwork or whatever else I have on my plate.

I usually try to run an errand outside of my home every day to clear the cobwebs and usually venture out early in the afternoon. Yesterday, as an example, I drove an hour each way to my bank in Michigan (I live in Canada) and met with some friends for a late lunch. The day before, it was shopping at the big local market, which I really like.

There will, of course, be email and phone calls when I arrive back and when those are dealt with I generally start making dinner for the 9 of us (that's right!J) See, I love to cook (hate to clean), command that job in the house because I find preparing a meal a great de-stresser.

If I'm too busy, someone else will whip something up, or, we'll order out. Maybe in our next interview you'll ask what my favorite dishes are J

I try to knock it off in the early evening, however, during product development periods (when I'm at my Virgo, workaholic best) I'll be at it 'til 10 or 11 p.m.

My sleep tonic is normally watching a good movie or documentary before retiring for the night.

7DayeBook – *Could you give some encouragement to new or aspiring ebook authors?*

Rick – Of course. There's no better way to finish up this interview than to have them read the following article.

Drive Your OWN Car Down the Information SuperHighway

aka: The "F" Theory

People are falling all over each other to fail on the Internet! (Not the usual introduction to a business article, but please hold that awful thought.)

Having owned several successful businesses over the years, I've come to learn, and sometimes the hard way, that in order to realize one's financial goals, one must take complete control of their own destiny. Hence, the title of this article. I also refer to this in the reverse as...

The "F" Theory: Few Find Financial Freedom Following

Consider this: There are more "Secrets to Riches on the Internet" courses than there are individual entrepreneurs actually making a good living on the Web.

And, there are more make-the-money-and-run, MLM scams successfully stalking prey on the Net, than network marketers actually making a full time living at working legitimate programs.

I repeat: People are falling all over each other to fail on the Internet!

One would think that with this new wide-open global frontier called the Internet that opportunity would abound and infinite possibilities would fill the computer screens of budding "netrepreneurs."

Well it does. But only if you approach it the right way.

Success on the Internet CAN be yours but it may not take the form of what you are now expecting or in some soon-to-come advertisement or flash/shock, hype-heavy opportunity website that happens to be spammed

in your face. In all likelihood, it won't even be something you search for in Yahoo or anywhere else.

Here's how it will happen for you:

- You will set your own course.
- You will choose your own speed.
- You will steer your own vehicle.
- You will win the race all by yourself.

It's really this simple. It reverts back to my "F" Theory, actually, the positive affirmation of it:

You WILL Drive Your Own Car Down the Information Super Highway.

YOU will take control of your destiny.

YOU will get behind the wheel and YOU will decide THE product that you want to offer the world.

YOU will put the selling process in gear and bring YOUR product to the attention of the worldwide Internet marketplace.

YOU will accept payment from YOUR customers and cut YOUR own paychecks, and not be dependant waiting a month or three for a commission check that may or may not arrive.

YOUR Product. YOUR customers. YOUR Sales. YOUR Business.

Sound far-fetched? Not at all. It's as simple as one decision.

Folks, JUST DECIDE TO DO IT! Once you decide, the road of possibilities becomes as wide as the Web itself. And once you decide, everything you need will flow to your goal. I have lived this truth countless times in my life.

Ok, enough philosophizing.

The big question is – Will You Need Help?

The big answer is – Yes You Will!

BUT BEWARE ... there are billions and billions of bits and bytes of scammy hype and misinformation out there. "Products" that confuse, frustrate and offer little or no true direction. There is a slew of self-ordained "guru's" out there who are preying on you, while praying for their next sale to come in.

There are private sites and marketing clubs that take your money and give you precious little useful, hard-core information, all the while trying to "back-end" you on other useless products they want to sell you.

Saddest thing of all, these shysters are really hurting honest "netizens", and there are millions now who are hungrily looking for truthful answers and solid solutions for this "Internet thing".

Don't people simply deserve the straight goods and the best information and resources on how to make money and earn a living from the World Wide Web?

Now, I create products that I sincerely believe will help people. I put together affiliate programs to promote them and provide thousands of people with an opportunity to both learn and earn income.

Some customers have no interest in reselling my products but I have MANY affiliates whose "product" IS representing a few select affiliate programs. Folks, these serious entrepreneurs are making hundreds, and even thousands of dollars per month (like, who couldn't quit their job and work at home making a couple of grand from 3 or 4 affiliate programs?) They do it THEIR WAY via a newsletter and/or well put together website.

Although I'm not suggesting this, my point is, THIS 'could' be your product.

But be it eBooks, or a newsletter, or resource site, or fly-fishing gear, you can and must create and sell Your Own Product!

Nothing makes my heart sing louder than to hear from a single mother who quit her day job, because she can now afford to work at home while raising her children just because she bought, and is following, the

lead I provided, in my first eBook, The Ezine Marketing Machine. And little makes me more proud than to be able to post numerous, like testimonials, on my websites.

So folks, it IS certainly possible!

You will NEVER fulfill your goal, be it striking it rich on the Internet, or just quitting your job to make a good living from home, by being a passenger.

YOU can Drive Your Own Car Down the Information SuperHighway!

I now wish you Godspeed and Best of Success!

eBook Author – Kristin Gilpatrick

Kristin Gilpatrick was born in Edgerton, Wis., to educators Robert and Barbara Gilpatrick.

She graduated from the University of Wisconsin-Eau Claire in 1990 with a double major in journalism and Spanish, having studied a semester in Valladolid, Spain. In college, her life-long passion for writing and history blossomed into a love for telling the stories of the "everyday" people who made history.

She put that passion to paper as a reporter for newspapers in Illinois and Wisconsin, winning nine press association awards along the way. Since 1997, she's been a magazine editor for the Credit Union Executives Society, Madison, Wis.

Her book is called *The Hero Next Door*™. You can find it at www.badgerbooks.com or at www.heronextdoor.org.

7DayeBook – *How did you get the idea for your ebook?*

Kristin – I've always been interested in World War II history and in the stories about every day people who took part in history so my books – about Wisconsinites who served well in war and continue to serve their community well afterwards—were a natural fit.

Also, I've been using the Internet at work for five years or more and feel that ebooks are the market of the future. I wanted to get my foot in the door to a different readership group from those buying it at bookstores, by offering my book in this format.

7DayeBook – *How much experience (if any) did you have in that area before deciding to write on the subject?*

Kristin – While I was "Internet-savvy," I really didn't know too much about ebooks except that Stephen King had given it a whirl. I just knew I didn't want to miss out on the opportunity to reach readers I might otherwise not get, in on the ground floor of a new way of publishing.

7DayeBook – *Why did you choose to publish through the Internet rather than by traditional means?*

Kristin – For the above stated reasons – though I still publish the book traditionally as well.

One of the benefits of ebook publishing is that your profit percentages/margins per book as an author are bigger (at least for me). Since I have a smaller, more regional publisher, his profit margin per book is bigger than it is in traditional selling venues (bookstores).

7DayeBook – *What challenges did you face with getting your book finished and ready for distribution on the web?*

Kristin – None too different from publishing it traditionally since I publish both ways.

I think the biggest stumbling block was fear that the book would be "stolen" and reprinted without permission since I've had that happen with some of my other online writing (articles).

However, I told myself that there's nothing stopping anyone from simply photocopying my traditionally published books as many times as they want either. So, the threat is really the same ... it would just be more immediate.

7DayeBook – *How long have you been writing and selling online?*

Kristin – About 1 year.

7DayeBook – *How much experience did you have with the WWW before you started selling your ebook?*

Kristin – I've been using WWW for about 5 years and am a magazine editor in my part-time job, for a publication that has both online and offline formats. So, luckily I was already pretty familiar with how the online world operates.

7DayeBook – *What are the biggest problems you have faced with selling your ebook?*

Kristin – Getting people to know it exists, which we still struggle with on a daily basis. You have to get the word out about your book in order to sell it.

7DayeBook – *Did you make mistakes that others could learn from?*

Kristin – I think my hesitation was a mistake; I also would do more upfront marketing and cross sell marketing. Perhaps pushing in my traditional books that an ebook version is available.

7DayeBook – *What advice would you give a new author starting out?*

Kristin – Trust your gut and don't be afraid to say "the book is done." (Letting a book go—saying that it's ready for "print"—is the hardest part of writing, at least for me.)

7DayeBook – *What daily activities would you suggest a new author engage in to market their ebook – understanding that they don't have a lot of time?*

Kristin – Obviously they should have a Web site to promote each book, or series of books that's well connected to search engines. Be sure the ebook is there but also be sure to cross sell the ebook through traditional marketing. One thing is that press releases about publishing an ebook can still get press (especially in smaller markets) because it's still so new. Also, at signings, I give out bookmarks or business cards that have my Web site right on them.

I've also been toying with the idea of doing an online book signing or author chat—complete with sending out invitations to people who've purchased one of my traditional books through my, or my publisher's, Web site ... that type of thing might generate some hype and ebook sales.

7DayeBook – *What would you do differently if you had it to do over again?*

Kristin – I would focus on promotion more, right from the beginning. It's hard for a writer to accept that writing is really only 30 percent of the work. **If you want anyone to read the book, you've got to be 70 percent a showman and salesman.**

7DayeBook – *What is your most successful means of marketing?*

Kristin – Word of mouth always blows away every other kind of marketing. Also, because I'm a former newspaper editor, I have a lot of luck with getting good press.

Otherwise, knowing your market and marketing to that specifically, is most important. For example, I'd never send a press release about my book to Better Homes & Gardens, but I send out regular notices and updates to military magazines, go to military shows to promote it, that sort of thing.

eBook Author – Kenneth Wajda

340 North Orchard Avenue
Canon City, CO 81212

ebook title: The Travel Photo Workshop Ebook (on CD)

Available – **http://TravelPhotoWorkshop.com/ebook.htm**

7DayeBook – *How did you get the idea for your ebook?*

Kenneth – I've been a professional photographer working at newspapers and freelancing to magazines for the past 15 years.

One day, a friend said whenever she goes on vacation, she never knows "where to put stuff", and asked me to show her. That was the idea for the ebook—to write a practical, easy-to-understand guide that is geared toward Travelers, not just photographers.

There's no talk of confusing f-stops and other off-putting technical jargon.

7DayeBook – *How much experience (if any) did you have in that area before deciding to write on the subject?*

Kenneth – My wife, also a photographer (that's how we met), and I were vacationing yearly and the last thing we wanted to do was bring large SLR cameras, the ones we lugged around at work.

So we always traveled with two tiny "point and shoot" cameras instead, an Olympus XA and Minolta AF-C. The difference is these cameras have extremely sharp lenses (no zooms). We shot professional slide film in them, Fuji Velvia, a slow-speed, fine-grain, film that is formulated to saturate colors. It's also the film of choice of most nature/travel photographers and many National Geographic photographers.

We were always so impressed with the travel photos, as were friends, that they became the obvious choice for the for the Travel Photo Workshop Ebook.

Photographically, I was very experienced.

7DayeBook – *Why did you choose to publish through the Internet rather than by traditional means?*

Kenneth – The choice to publish electronically was made simply as a way to self-publish. The ebook is also sold at art shows and other venues including travel agencies. (It's not offered in photo stores, ironically, because I don't advocate buying the latest equipment and accessories.)

The ebook is aimed at "doing more with less". I explain how many of the new cameras have poor lenses.

"How many one-hour photo labs are responsible for bad photos – not the photographer?"

Unfortunately, retail stores don't appreciate talk like that so I knew it would be hard to get "traditional" distribution for the book.

It's funny, I want to get a rubber stamp that says BANNED IN PHOTO STORES!

7DayeBook – *What challenges did you face with getting your book finished and ready for distribution on the web?*

Kenneth – At first it was written in a program called Authorware, but the ebook would only play on Windows computers. That was a problem. So I had to rewrite it as a Word document and then convert it to a PDF document so it could be read on Mac computers as well.

7DayeBook – *How long have you been writing and selling online?*

Kenneth – I've been writing travel articles and other short non-fiction pieces online for the past two years. I have another ebook on buying quality used cars for little money titled, "The Great Cheap Used Car Ebook" – it's available at **http://greatcheapusedcar.esmartweb.com/**

7DayeBook – *How much experience did you have with the WWW before you started selling your ebook?*

Kenneth – Quite a bit. I know my way around the web and computers very well, though I'm not a geek. I know what I need to know...and I know where to look for help to troubleshoot.

7DayeBook – *What are the biggest problems you have faced with selling your ebook?*

Kenneth – Getting the word out. The web is so vast right now, that it takes a lot to get seen and heard. You're like a small pebble falling into the ocean and you want your ripple to be seen.

7DayeBook – *Did you make mistakes that others could learn from?*

Kenneth – The big one was having it in an incompatible format for Macs. Write it in Word and publish as a PDF file so your book can be read in Adobe Acrobat Reader.

7DayeBook – *What advice would you give a new author starting out?*

Kenneth – Write something that you believe in. I take photographs for a living and I love to bring back travel photos that amaze people. That's a great feeling.

It's also rewarding if they can learn to do the same in their travels. So, this ebook was easy for me to write. I wasn't writing on some topic that I thought would just make the big bucks.

Even the used car ebook came from the fact that my wife and I have routinely purchased great used cars over the years for very little money. The car I drive now is a 1988 Subaru Wagon that was bought at a yard sale (no kidding) from a woman who had to sell it before she moved to Germany for $1250 with only 70,000 miles. It's up to 155,000 now and still going strong—it surely beats car payments! The deals are out there.

I just wrote about my way of looking for those deals.

7DayeBook – *How profitable is your ebook?*

Kenneth – Sales online are not as great as I would like, but I'm not pouring money into advertising, either. I make some sales off my website, but most of them come from referrals from the art shows.

7DayeBook – *What daily activities would you suggest a new author engage in to market their ebook – understanding that they don't have a lot of time?*

Kenneth – Do other things that are of interest to web readers. I have a Travel Photo Workshop Newsletter that offers tips for great travel photographs.

It's at http://kennethwajda.com/newsevents.htm

Another thing, I created a screensaver, The Travel Photo Workshop Screensaver

http://download.cnet.com/downloads/0-1461912-100-5739582.html?tag=st.dl.10001-103-1.lst-4-11.5739582

It contains 12 beautiful travel scenic photographs and I offer it as a free download at Download.com. That screen-saver has been downloaded (as of this morning) 8,975 times since April 26, 2001. At the end of the photos is a slide that gives info on the Travel Photo Workshop Ebook.

I have another screensaver coming out called the "Travel Photo Workshop Photo Tips Screensaver," that actually offers tips as well as photos, for free download.

And again, there's a tag screen at the end promoting the website.

7DayeBook – *If you had to do it all over again what would you do the same?*

Kenneth – I'd write the same books, the ones I believe in. I wouldn't go to the "Getrich quick" genre, that's for sure.

7DayeBook – *What is your most successful means of marketing?*

Kenneth – The free screensaver at Download.com has brought the most traffic to the website.

eBook author – KENNETH C. MORRELL

Fiction: "Counter Power"
Nonfiction: "From Horses to Spies"
Children's Fiction: "Freddie Grows Up"
Short stories: "Beware! Danger Ahead"

7DayeBook – *How did you get the idea for your ebook?*

Ken – My first effort in writing was an autobiography about my career in the US Air Force. I wanted to leave a history for my descendents. After writing the story- titled "Inside Air Force Intelligence", although some time had passed, I sent it to the Pentagon for review.

The book included a considerable amount of previously classified information. I knew I could talk or write about anything they didn't edit out.

When this book had been written, my wife suggested I should write about my life before joining the air force. I thought this was a good idea, and wrote "The Early Years."

While writing this second book, I began submitting the first book to conventional publishers attempting to have it printed. I wasn't having any success and by the time the second book was finished, I decided to self publish a limited number of copies for family and friends. I combined the two books into one, "From Horses to Spies".

7DayeBook – *How much experience (if any) did you have in that area before deciding to write on the subject?*

Ken – The first book, an autobiography of course, was based upon my life in the USAF. Most of that time was spent in clandestine intelligence collection work – human source intelligence collection or HUMINT. A great deal of that time was spent as a Case Officer, working with and directing foreign agents.

This experience and background was of great assistance in my later fiction books (except Freddie Grows Up).

7DayeBook – *Why did you choose to publish through the Internet rather than by traditional means?*

Ken – I initially did try to publish by traditional means, however the countless submissions, rejections, time wasted and cost dealing with publishers became very frustrating!

7DayeBook – *What challenges did you face with getting your book finished and ready for distribution on the web?*

Ken – I never realized how many web sites there are, which do web publishing in varying degrees. Some charge fees, contracts and time periods are different, and requirements for submission are quite varied. But it all comes down to what is required to write a book, persistence, patience and a good editor!

7DayeBook – *How long have you been writing and selling online?*

Ken – I have been writing for about four years, and been selling online for six months.

7DayeBook – *What are the biggest problems you have faced with selling your ebooks?*

Ken – Getting people to the site. There are so many out there now, that the hits on any but the most well known sites are low.

7DayeBook – *Did you make mistakes that others could learn from?*

Ken – Make sure your book is well edited.

Thoroughly check out the various book sites on the web. Are they easily identified on the various search listings under book publishers, ebooks, e-publishers, etc.?

Be sure to look at the site and see what other kinds of books are listed and only go after sites that attract people who would be interested in your book.

Finally, definitely read the submission requirements and contract thoroughly!

7DayeBook – *What advice would you give a new author starting out?*

Ken – Develop a subject you want to write about; research it thoroughly; start writing – and make sure you enjoy putting in the time required and stick to it!

7DayeBook – *What daily activities would you suggest a new author engage in to market their ebook – understanding they don't have a lot of time?*

Ken – My e-publisher has sent out to his authors, examples of small "chits" which can be used as examples for bookmarks, to print and hand out to friends.

He has also suggested contacting local newspapers and newsletters to provide them with information about the author's work and, of course, the web site address for inclusion in their publications.

EXAMPLE:

LOCAL AUTHOR
THREE NEW BOOKS & A SHORT STORY
By: Kenneth C. Morrell
Where: www.YOURWEBSITE.com
Click on Fiction – then "COUNTER POWER"
Next try Children's Fiction – and "FREDDIE GROWS UP"
Then go to Non Fiction – click on "FROM HORSES TO SPIES"
For a Short Story – try "BEWARE ! DANGER AHEAD"

*****Hope you enjoy these three books*****

7DayeBook – *What would you do differently if you had it to do over again?*

Ken – I would definitely skip the paper publishers and go directly to the e-publishers!

7DayeBook – *If you had it to do over again what would you do the same?*

Ken – I would write! I would also use the style, which has worked for me, i.e., develop an idea, start writing and let it flow.

For me, outlining before starting doesn't work. I do write down ideas as they come to mind—sometimes to add later in the story I'm working on, or even, a later book!

7DayeBook – Ken made one additional point in the interview I thought you would benefit from – here it is...

Ken – One problem ebook publishers have is the fear some people have of using their credit cards on the Internet. I mentioned to my publisher that he should come up with an alternative means of paying. He emailed back to me that his accountant had mentioned the same point.

In addition to credit card payments, the site now has a way to send payment by mail, but still have your ebook downloaded to an email address.

Bonus Report – Marketing "Guru" Jay Conrad Levinson Speaks!

The original master of Online Marketing offers valuable insights, tips and his priceless advice to help individuals compete effectively with much larger organizations.

Jay Conrad Levinson is the author of the best-selling marketing series in history, "Guerrilla Marketing," plus 24 other business books. His guerrilla concepts have influenced marketing so much that today his books appear in 37 languages.

He writes a monthly column for Entrepreneur Magazine, articles for Inc. Magazine, a syndicated column for newspapers and magazines and online columns published monthly on the Microsoft and GTE websites.

Two of Jay's books, "Online Marketing Weapons" and "Guerrilla Marketing Online", are invaluable to anyone who wants to learn the right ways to market any business or product on the Internet!

Jay Conrad Levinson
Guerrilla Marketing International
P.O. Box 1336
Mill Valley, CA 94942
Email: GMINTL@aol.com

Check out Jay's sites:

www.gmarketing.com and the NEW and improved www.JayConradLevinson.com!

Find out the latest and greatest tactics and tools for guerrilla marketing on and offline. The daily email tips are superb and Jay can turn anyone into a highly trained and effective marketer in a very short period of time.

If you don't listen to anyone else's advice about marketing online – listen to Jay!

7DayeBook – *Jay we want to thank you very much for agreeing to spend some time with us today.*

Jay – It's my pleasure.

7DayeBook – *Where do you see the world of online marketing going for the "little guy" – the person you call the Guerrilla Marketer.*

Jay – The concept of online marketing for small business is going to make everything easier for small business owners and entrepreneurs, because frequently these people have as much experience as huge Fortune 500 companies. Since this is a new technology – everybody is learning by doing – and they are all learning at the same time, the web really levels the playing field.

The smaller organization – even one person – can deal with the changes online much more quickly than the big organizations.

Also, insight in how to use the internet is much more in favor of the smaller operation, because of all the quality information that is being put out now, in the form of excellent books, and online newsletters and ezines.

If a person really wants to market online, the information is out there and it is totally up-to-date – you just have to go out, get it and most importantly, implement it!

One important word of caution right now though – I always tell everyone you have to know marketing before you can understand Internet Marketing. Now you can learn them both at the same time, but you have to understand sound, proven marketing strategies before you can market online… and that starts with a marketing plan!

7DayeBook – *But Jay with such a glut of information out on the web, how does someone who doesn't know marketing, separate the people who know what they are talking about, from the people who are just parroting what they have heard from other people? How do they know what information is real?*

Jay – Boy, that varies all the time! I write books just to answer that question. I write newsletters and magazine columns, just to answer that question.

I think the way to learn about marketing is to understand that there is more great information out there than ever before… and anybody who doesn't want to take the time to learn that information, is not going to succeed in online marketing. As you learn you will see – the principles will become apparent to you – and you will empower yourself

to make the decisions about what is, and what is not, good information.

Also, keep in mind that online marketing is a process of experimentation and constant improvement. Mistakes can sometimes be the greatest teachers. I know they have been for me.

But understand this – whatever businesses you are in, you are also in the marketing business. Whether you sell a book, a product or a service, you not only sell that book, product or service but you are also a marketing person for that.

Any businessperson who does not understand that concept not only won't succeed – they *can't* succeed, because it physically can't happen... because making marketing work is an ongoing process of learning and experimentation.

7DayeBook – *What's the first thing people should understand about marketing online?*

Jay – When small businesses think about marketing online they usually think about having a website, but it doesn't have to be the first thing they do. If they join forums and newsgroups, and other special interest groups they can participate in those forums and provide value and build themselves up as experts in their fields.

They can then use email to build relationships with other people who can help them sell their product, service or information, whether they buy directly or refer other people to buy.

This activity doesn't require that you have a website.

You can also participate in chat rooms that specialize in what you sell or what you make.

There are companies out there that would like to have you offer to host conferences for them. AOL does a whole lot of conferences and they are always looking for people to host conferences without blatant selling.

Your ability to host a conference doesn't require a website.

It comes down to realizing that there are a lot of websites out there that need quality content and if you can give it to them they will give you the exposure you need.

You can post articles on the websites of others and they will give you a paragraph at the end where you can say something about yourself, your product or book and direct people either to a site or to call or email you.

7DayeBook – *Now how would you go about finding those places to post, host or share content?*

Jay – Start searching within your industry and you will find companies that have websites and you will realize that they could really use a great article for their site. Of course a lot of them will say yes to posting that article, because you write about what they do! You will provide valuable content for free.

7DayeBook – *And they need valuable content!*

Jay – Right! Now it is hard to find companies that will pay you outright for these articles, but you should use them to get exposure – as a free marketing device.

You can post the same article to a lot of sites and at the bottom of the article you can direct people to you. And since you are the EXPERT (you wrote the article) people will come to you.

Another way to get exposure – ***and by the way these are all ways so far that don't cost any money*** – is to use the classified ad sections of the web.

7DayeBook – *Are those the same thing as Free For All Links (FFA pages)?*

Jay – No, classified ad sites are different. Some are paid and some are free. You won't get through to a lot of people – but you will get through to a lot MORE people than if you didn't do anything and, again, this doesn't cost you any money. You will get results if you are willing to resubmit your ads every day.

This can really help you when you are just starting out and if you decide later on that you have other ways to better invest your time then you can stop. But in the beginning, especially if you don't have a lot of money, this is a viable way to market your book, product or service.

7DayeBook – *Where do you find these classified ad sites?*

Jay – One is called www.buysellbid.com but you can also go to a search engine such as Google and just put in "classified ads" and start from there. But there are lots of sections that are available to you. Some are free and some cost, but all are low cost when compared with other means of marketing.

7DayeBook – *What else can people do?*

Jay – Now we have gotten to the point where someone would need a website. But I want to point out all the things you can do *without* a website.

Now I know a website is the first thing many people think about with marketing online, but I thought it was really important that they see there are other marketing tools available before we move on.

7DayeBook – *All the things we've talked about so far before the website do 2 things for you. First, it sets you up as the expert in your field and, secondly, these activities are driving people to you or your website.*

Is that right?

Jay – Exactly.

7DayeBook – *Now with regard to your website – and there is a lot of debate on this – there is a major shift on the Internet right now to one and two page websites, as opposed to the old model of having a 50 – 100 – 200 page website.*

What do you think about this?

Jay – I think that the, short to the point, websites are the future because the web is getting so crowded that people who show up to your website will give you about 3 to 8 seconds of their attention before they surf away.

If they don't see what's in it for them, in a way that catches and holds their attention, they are out of there!

Do you know about the monkey in the cage?

If you put a monkey in a cage with a vat of Jell-O and a ladder – what's on the monkey's mind?

7DayeBook – *What's that?*

Jay – Where's the Banana! <grin>

And if you then switch out the Jell-O for water and put a bell and a mirror in the monkey's cage – what's on the monkey's mind?

7DayeBook – *What?*

Jay – Where's the Banana!

Although your website visitors are not monkey's, what's on their mind? What's in it for them – their banana!

You see people only care about what they are interested in. A one page or a two page website lets people know right up front whether they should give you their attention or not. If they should, then that type of website structure holds their attention longer and pulls them deeper into your sales letter.

If not, then they can go search for their banana elsewhere!

They are not willing to hunt for their banana either. A lot of sites hide the banana deeper within the site rather than plainly displaying it on the home page.

If your visitors can't find what they want, and that interests them immediately, they will go someplace else.

7DayeBook – *When you say, that immediately, what comes directly into my mind, is the headline at the top of the page.*

Jay – That and the sub-headlines. Anything that is clearly communicated to them – but understand, you can't communicate a whole lot, so you have to hit the main point very quickly or you've lost them.

I'm not saying you can't give people a lot of options, you just have to make it perfectly clear up front what is in it for them so they'll stick around to explore the options! Also, make sure the site is not about you, your site should be all about the visitor and their needs.

The old way was to hide the banana and hope they found it.

Now you have to put the banana on the front page so they see that first.

7DayeBook – *With everything evolving and changing so fast, how does somebody spot change and adapt to it quickly in their marketing online?*

Jay – They have to subscribe to the right publications – offline and online – because ezines, magazines and newsletters stay up to date much more than any book ever could.

You should engage in something called the "weekly surf," where every week you spend an hour just surfing around looking at what others inside and outside your industry are doing. Follow the links and see where they take you and see what ideas you get.

This will really help you stay abreast of what others are doing as well as pick up on new and exciting trends in marketing online.

When you find something that looks like it is working and will make an improvement to your online business – USE IT! ACT!

Don't just sit there and say "that's nice"- do something with it!

7DayeBook – *What else would you recommend, that someone who was really willing to take action, do on a weekly basis to keep themselves and their product constantly moving in a positive direction?*

Jay – First, they should start joining targeted newsgroups and forums and consistently following along in them and contributing in a valuable way. Your job at this point is to build relationships and build your mailing list of people who respect you and want more information from you as it becomes available.

Building this permission based email list is the ultimate goal of any online marketer. In the future this is how you will get people to your site to read your sales letter, sign up for your new service or buy a product from you.

People want convenience and that is part of the reason for people reacting well to these one page websites. They are in a hurry and want what they want in an easily digestible form.

7DayeBook – *Now in reference to that convenience factor.*

Would you agree that so much information is available for free on the Internet and people could eventually track it all down if they wanted to invest the time. Isn't convenience the reason they pay $30, $40, even $50 or more for someone else to digest that information and give it to them in a way they can use almost immediately?

Jay – That is the key to what is happening and why it is happening online.

If you can provide information and knowledge for people, whether in book form, personal coaching, a seminar or something else, they will pay you for it so they can get the information quickly, solve their problem and move on.

7DayeBook – *Now let's say someone just created a product like an ebook, or a newsletter, or any type of product they want to launch – what should they do?*

Jay – The first thing I'd tell them to do is realize they will, ultimately need a website. That is the place to bring everything together.

So first, plan why you want a website?

What do you hope to accomplish with that website and put it down in writing.

This is the start of your online marketing plan – the goal for your website!

It's not enough to put your name up on the web with a bunch of pretty pictures.

"Why are you going to take the time, trouble and expense of going online with a website?" is the first question you must ask.

It all begins with planning – and in some cases you might not need a website (though most people reading this will).

Once you decide you need a website and what the purpose of the site is the next step is to determine what the content will be.

Should the content just be to sell people and have them make a buying decision right then, or should it be good information that answers questions?

The goal of your site will determine what content is necessary.

The next thing they should address is the design. Since people show up to the site in the "stay or bail" mode – meaning they will give you 3-8 seconds to decide whether to "stay" and check you out or "bail" to another site – your site must be designed in a way to catch them.

The next thing you must understand, this is a media that *involves* people.

How are you going to involve people with your website?

Will you have them sign up for a free newsletter?

Do you want them to enter a sweepstakes?

You have to start a dialogue with people.

7DayeBook – *And really that involvement is where you begin to build the relationship, right?*

Jay – Yes, and in the process you are getting permission from them to follow up with valuable information later.

Anyone who gets involved with you and your site is really giving you permission to continue being marketed to, as long as your messages meet their needs and you provide value.

Now after you've done that, you have to produce all this and it is actually pretty easy to produce a basic website.

If you don't want to hire someone there are software programs that make it pretty easy to set up a site – you don't have to be a programmer if you have some basic computer skills and understand how to use a word processor.

Those are the things that most everybody does to some degree. I have found, though, they're not too good at the planning part…

and they're pretty good at content because they realize it is important…

they do their best at design…

they're not sure about involvement or how to do it – though if you adopt the mindset that you must continually strive to get the name and email of every visitor, you will figure out the best involvement strategies for your particular site…

and finally they are able to produce the site with easy-to-use software.

7DayeBook – *And then once they've got that, they continue to do what you talked about earlier, which is the hosting, posting, forums, newsgroups, chat rooms, classified ads and search engines to start driving traffic across that site and keep the stream of surfers coming?*

Jay – Yes.

And to take it even further, the main area people fall down in after they have gone through these five steps of planning, content, design, involvement and production, is follow up.

This is so important.

You have to find ways to bring people back or to keep putting your name and expertise in front of them and not take them for granted.

7DayeBook – *Would following up with a newsletter or a sequential autoresponder be an example of what you're talking about there?*

Jay – Yes, and the more personalized you can make it, both in content and appearance, the better you will do and the better results you will encounter.

I'm blown away when I get an email from Amazon that tells me "Hey, these three new books came out and based on what you've bought in the past we thought you might be interested." That is absolutely marvelous and anyone can take those same principals and apply them if they take the time to build their list and their relationships the right way.

In fact, people are actually very impressed with the fact that a live human being sent them an email rather than just having an autoresponder.

7DayeBook – *Yep... that really freaks people out sometimes, when they realize, "Oh wow – a live human being sent me this email!"*

Jay – You bet! And the next area that has got to be addressed – and this is where a lot of people fail with websites – and that is with "promotion".

You have to realize that most people live in two worlds – the offline and online worlds – and if you are doing any offline promotion you *must* include and promote your online presence in it!

If you know your website converts people to buyers or gets them to take the action you want them to take, then you have to devote a large portion of your time and advertising budget to getting people to show up to the site!

The idea of promoting your site all over the place is pretty darn crucial. Take every opportunity to promote it.

7DayeBook – *But you don't agree with any type of spamming, do you?*

Jay – NO! Spamming we are totally against, because it does a lot more harm than good and doesn't accomplish your ultimate objective, which is to create a relationship.

7DayeBook – *So what is the third thing people usually miss out on?*

Jay – The final area people miss the boat on is maintenance.

If you realize that a website is like a brand new baby – you have to change it, feed it, nurture it and maintain it. You can't treat it like a magazine ad that you run once. A website needs constant attention.

To help people remember this I teach people the rule of "thirds" and it is critical to understand this principle if you want to succeed.

Here's how it works – If you are going to go online, determine how much of a budget you are going to have, in terms of time **and** money.

1/3 of your budget should go to developing your site;

1/3 in promoting your site;

1/3 in maintaining your site and keeping it fresh!

Most people invest 3/3 into just *developing* their site and then wonder why it fails!

7DayeBook – *So they blow all their money getting the "pretty pictures"?*

Jay – Exactly!

It's a good looking site and everything about it might be good, except nobody knows it's there. If people do visit the site and are fascinated by it, but come back and see nothing has changed – they'll never come back again!

7DayeBook – *Well let me ask you – that's a really good point if you are operating a content or a reference site, but how does this maintenance rule apply to someone who has got one of these one page websites that's really effective, and all of their direct marketing experience tells them, "If it's not broken don't fix it."?*

Jay – In that case – leave it alone!

But remember, you will have to change the site eventually as technology and surfer behavior changes.

That brings up a very interesting point.

The most amazing thing in my career – and I've seen this more frequently than I like – is when I find a client who needs marketing help and he shows me the things that worked and I ask them, "Why did you stop doing it!?"

Sometimes something works so well you won't have to change it for a very long time, but you should also be careful to avoid complacency too.

7DayeBook – *Well Jay we can't thank you enough for taking the time to give all of our readers some valuable insight into marketing online.*

If they just follow the basic steps you've laid out here with their website, hosting, posting, chat, search engines and more they are well on their way to being effective online guerrilla marketers.

Thanks!

Jay – Thank you. It has been a pleasure.

7DayeBook – *For more information on Jay Conrad Levinson log on to*

www.gmarketing.com and the NEW and improved www.JayConradLevinson.com!

Find out the latest and greatest tactics and tools for guerrilla marketing on and offline. The daily email tips are superb and Jay can turn anyone into a highly trained and effective marketer in a very short period of time.

If you don't listen to anyone else's advice about marketing online – listen to Jay!

Bonus Report – Accept Credit Cards Online Without Breaking the Bank

Anyone who ever thought about starting an online business will ask the same question at some time during their quest for Internet millions – "How do I accept credit cards?"

Since over 90% of all transactions on the Internet involve using a credit card, your business will ultimately fail unless you allow your online customers to use plastic. The problem for most small businesses and "micropreneurs" involves the high cost of setting up and maintaining a credit card merchant account.

With startup fees ranging from $200 to $500, minimum monthly fees of at least $40 to $50, plus per transaction fees and a percentage of sales, no wonder most fledgling businesses never make it off the ground?

Add in credit checks, 48 month service contracts, expensive equipment purchases or leasing, and required financial statements that make you feel like you just applied for "Top-Secret" national security status!

Most people throw up their hands and give up before they even get started. Most people can't or won't fork over hundreds of dollars and obligate themselves to years of service contracts, just to test out an idea online.

Fortunately at least one company responded to this problem with unique solutions that enable online information sellers to accept credit cards at a fraction of those high startup costs with no long-term commitment, no equipment purchases and zero minimum monthly fees.

ClickBank (http://www.clickbank.com)

For a $50 one-time fee ClickBank enables online ebook sellers to not only accept credit cards, but provide instant delivery of their books to online purchasers.

ClickBank allows any merchant to accept all the major credit cards. The online merchant simply adds a purchase link to their site, the customer clicks the link, fills in their payment information and the credit card gets authorized on the spot.

Once the card gets approved, ClickBank redirects the buyer to a page that enables them to download the ebook, software, or other product they just purchased.

The buyer gets an email receipt from ClickBank with the details of the transaction. The seller also gets an email from ClickBank letting them know a transaction took place, along with the buyer's name, email address and state.

ClickBank mails checks every two weeks for sales made through your account, minus 7.5% of each transaction and a $1 fee.

ClickBank also charges a $2.50 fee for each check they send out, but sellers can pick the minimum amount they want to make before a check gets issued.

ClickBank also makes it easy to recruit and pay others to help sell your product through your own affiliate program. ClickBank provides the tools for setting up affiliate links, tracking sales and takes care of paying them every two weeks.

Overall, ClickBank represents an excellent option for anyone who wants to test their hand at selling online information without spending hundreds of dollars on credit card processing for a product that may or may not sell.

Bonus Report – Web Hosting: More Affordable Than Ever!

When Jim launched his first website way back in the "dark ages" of 1997 he began paying almost $150 a month in hosting and data transfer charges.

His web host watched how many files he uploaded, like a hawk, and took fiendish glee in sending him large invoices every single month… but all that changed for the better!

With the advent of really inexpensive and reliable web hosting, nobody has an excuse for not getting their own website to promote their product, ebook or business.

Host Save

Host Save, another low price hosting company, delivers a wide range of services for only $7.95 per month.

They offer email accounts, website statistics, autoresponders and a cgi bin for using such scripts as "form mail" which allows you to put email and other forms on your website.

Host Save also uses a nifty feature that makes it very simple to password protect a directory, so you only allow access to certain files through a web browser, if the user knows the correct name and password.

If you operate a small site, where your world won't end and your children won't starve if the site gets slow for an hour or two, then this might represent a great hosting option for you.

www.Name2Host.com

Name2Host offers perhaps the absolute best in "cheap" web hosting.

For $15-35 they will register your domain name and host your site for a year.

Name2Host offers email services and a good bit of data transfer, but nothing else unless you want to pay to upgrade your service.

With all that said, sometimes cheap really doesn't pay well. Unless you know how to act as your own webmaster, you might do better to pay $10 more a month to use a hosting service with live people you can call for help. You'll forget all about any money you saved, when your site goes down with nobody around to help you get it back up!

www.DotEasy.com

True $0 Web Hosting... DotEasy will give you a year's worth of hosting if you buy a domain name through them for $25

Not a bad deal if you're just getting started!

Bonus Report – How an eBook "Cover" Can Skyrocket Sales!

In 1999, Vaughan Davidson sold his catalogue business because he knew the Internet held his future. After a period of learning and research about the Internet, he started his business, **Killer Covers (http://www.killercovers.com)**, in mid 2000 in response to a need most e-authors didn't even realize they had – the need for an ebook "cover".

This particular industry on the Internet has grown with amazing speed, and Vaughan is considered by many to be, "the cover designer to the stars!"

He has designed covers for many of the most successful ebooks of all time and he has graciously agreed to share some of his expert advice with us!

By the way – Vaughan designed the cover for our ebook and we think he did an excellent job!

7DayeBook – *Why does someone need an ebook "cover" – I thought the whole point of ebooks was to save the printing costs?*

Vaughan – First off, there are no printing costs with an ebook cover. An ebook cover is just a 3d style graphical image of your ebook that sits on your web site.

Why does someone need an ebook "cover"? Simple. The internet is predominantly a visual medium. Your customers like to see and understand what they are buying. When your customer sees a 3D style image of an ebook on our screen, they instantly understand what it is.

We have all seen a book before, but we have not all seen or an ebook. Some people don't even know what an ebook is. But when they see the 3D image, it all makes sense. And people only buy things that make sense to them.

7DayeBook – *Who should get an ebook cover done?*

Vaughan – As I said earlier, an ebook cover is a 3D style image of your ebook. They are also referred to as 'Virtual Covers'.

Who should get a cover done or do it themselves? Anyone who is selling any kind of ebook or information package on the Internet! Here is the reason why....

Because people DO judge a book by its cover!

Don't believe me? Go into any bookstore and look around. Nine times out of ten it is the cover design that will first draw your eye to a particular book. It's at that moment your first impressions are formed and the sale is made..... or lost!

The same is true on the Internet, even more so. That's because everything on the Net is two-dimensional. If you want to make a good first impression, to build trust, and create value in your customers mind, then you have to present your product in a way your customer can relate to.

You have to present it in a way that makes your customer want to reach into their screen and pick it up. If you can do that, make the product jump and say, "Hey! Look at me! I'm real – buy me now!" then you will make more sales.

It's as simple as that.

7DayeBook – *Can't I just make an ebook cover myself using PhotoShop or PaintShop and skip the cost of hiring someone?*

Vaughan – Absolutely, particularly if you already have an understanding of how to use software programs like PhotoShop or PaintShop. Or you could take the time to learn how to use them properly.

7DayeBook – *What makes a great – truly outstanding – ebook cover?*

Vaughan – One that sells a lot of ebooks. After all, that is why you create a cover in the first place.

What makes a cover sell? Allowing your customers eye to flow over the cover and understand what the ebook is about – Quickly!

If you have a cover that is overcrowded with images and text that is all screaming for attention, you will lose your customer.

When I design a cover I pick the most important message I want to get across. That could be the title, the sub title, the guarantee, a bullet point, or even an image. Once I have identified that message, I then let everything else *support* that message... not compete with it.

7DayeBook – *What advice would you give someone who wanted to make their own ebook cover?*

Vaughan – Think about whom you want to buy your ebook. Think about their likes and dislikes. What colors will motivate them to buy.

What images or colors could you use on the cover that will reinforce the message of your sales copy.

It is also important to remember that the cover you use to sell your ebook will say a lot about the quality of that ebook. Get that wrong and you could end up losing sales.

7DayeBook – *How much does an ebook cover cost if you hire someone to do it?*

Vaughan – Like most things, the price of an ebook cover varies considerably. Also like most things, you usually get what you pay for.

I have seen ebook covers for as little as $20, but to be honest, you could probably do a better job yourself.

If you look around you can easily find graphic designers charging $300 or more. These designers usually don't specialize in ebook covers, they are more interested in corporate logos and letterheads. But they are always happy to create a cover if asked.

The interesting thing to note is that the covers these high-priced graphic designers create usually are no better (and sometimes worse) than the covers from a designer specializing only in cover design service – like **Killer Covers.**

At **Killer Covers** I only do covers. They are my specialty and as such I only charge $149.50.

7DayeBook – *Do you have any tips (like a top 10 list) for anyone who wants to make their own cover?*

Vaughan – Absolutely – here is my "TOP 10" list of ebook cover design Tips!

1. Know your customer and what type of cover will appeal to them.

2. Before you start, create a list of the title, subtitle, bullet points, and even the guarantee you want to include on the cover.

3. Decide the most important message you want to get across and how you plan to get it across.

4. Also before you start, collect any images you wish to include in your cover and make sure you are legally allowed to use them.

5. Look around a bookstore or library and make a list of any covers you like, and what it is you like about them.

6. When you are designing your cover, try not to squeeze too much onto it. The more you put on, the less readable it will be.

7. Use fonts that are easily readable. Some of the more artistic fonts become unreadable when you wrap the cover into a 3D shape.

8. Contrast is important, so avoid using a white background on your cover if the background on your site is also white.

9. If you want your cover to have "life" avoid using all dark colors.

10. Lastly, remember the old K.I.S.S. rule – "Keep It Simple Stupid!"

7DayeBook – *Do you have any tips (like a top 10 list) for anyone who wants to hire someone to make their cover?*

Vaughan – Absolutely!

1. First and foremost, check out their work. Do you like the covers they have designed for other people?
2. Ask around. If you see a cover on a site you like, ask the site owner who designed it and what it was like to work with that designer?
3. Check out the references or testimonials on the designer's site. Do they link back to the site of the person who wrote the testimonial? That way you can see the cover on their site and how it fits.
4. Will the designers style appeal to your target customer?
5. Does their work leap off the screen and say, "Buy Me!" If the samples on their site don't say that, then you can bet the cover they produce for you won't either.
6. What is their turnaround time? Or in other words, how long will it take to deliver the completed cover to you, and does that fit your time frame?
7. On their order form, what questions do they ask you? Do they ask enough questions to get a real feel for what you and your customers are after?
8. What price do they charge? Does it fit with your budget?

9. What guarantee do they offer? What you need to look for is a, "we will keep working until you get a cover you like, or your money back" guarantee. Anything else and you could end up paying for a cover you are not happy with.
10. Who else have they designed for, and do those customers buy regularly?

7DayeBook – *Can you give us some examples of truly outstanding ebook covers you've done or seen and a brief explanation as to why each is so great?*

Vaughan – Probably the easiest way to see examples of my best work is to pop along to this page I have created especially for your readers.... CLICK HERE to see examples of Vaughan's work. **(http://www.killercovers.com/gallery.php)**

On this page you will see not only my latest work, but also some of my favorite and very best ebook covers.

7DayeBook – *How should people contact you if they are interested in finding out more about you and your business?*

Vaughan – The easiest way to contact me is to visit my site by clicking here =====> **Killer Covers!**

(http://www.killercovers.com)

Bonus Interview – Joe Vitale Speaks

Author of Spiritual Marketing

By
Charles Burke
(Command More Luck)
May 3, 2001

Command More Luck (CML): Today we're talking with a man who is a successful author and Internet businessman, and who is also legendary as a publicist and copywriter, Joe Vitale. You can find his main website at http://www.mrfire.com

Joe, thanks for being with us today.

Joe Vitale: Well thank you. It's a great treat, a great honor, and I'm excited.

CML: For readers who may not be familiar with your name, could you give us a bit of background about yourself and your business and career?

Joe: Well, I'm a full-time marketing consultant and author of some eight or ten books including a couple of best-selling eBooks. I have several audiotape programs including a best-selling one with Nightingale-Conant called "The Power of Outrageous Marketing." And my most recent book is called "Spiritual Marketing." The one before that was the only book only written on P.T. Barnum called "There's a Customer Born Every Minute." And I wrote "The Seven Lost Secrets of Success" and the "AMA Complete Guide to Small Business Advertising" and "Cyberwriting" and "Turbocharge Your Writing" and you know, on and on.

So there you go in a nutshell.

CML: Your books on copywriting, in particular, "Hypnotic Writing" and "Advanced Hypnotic Writing," have helped me tremendously with my sales letter writing.

Joe: That's good to know.

CML: How did you get into copywriting?

Joe: Oh boy! What a great question. How did I get into copywriting? Probably because I needed a copywriter. So I learned to do it for myself. Now, obviously I've been a writer for a long time. I've been writing since I was a teenager, and when I started getting my work published, I quickly learned that publishers don't know anything about marketing, and that if I wanted to get these books marketed I had to be responsible for it. So I just started learning the craft.

There were a couple of books. *The Robert Collier Letter Book* changed my life as a copywriter, and I became much more powerful as a writer after reading that book. That, and the works of John Caples, and just learning it on my own and applying it to my own needs. Then as I became successful, people started coming to me and saying, "Hey, will you do the same thing?"

So I more or less evolved into being a copywriter.

CML: Did that take a pretty good length of time, learning copywriting as a craft?

Joe: That's hard to answer because I already had such an extensive background as a writer. I had written a play that was produced in Houston back in 1979, and I learned a lot about dialog that I used in my copywriting.

Also, I had written a novel, and I learned a lot about storytelling that also goes into my copywriting.

I had written some articles and was a journalist, and I learned about factual writing, which goes into my copywriting. So that was kind of a lifetime experience. I can't say it took me 20 years or two years. It was always learning to be a better writer and then learning how to apply that to the craft of copywriting.

CML: And I suppose you're still digging around for stuff to learn.

Joe: I'm always digging around. Some people are astonished. I'm sitting in this beautiful library that I own – there are like 5,000 books here – and maybe a fifth of them are all on marketing and copywriting and becoming a better writer; they think, "Well, don't you know it all?"

And, no, I'm nowhere near it. I mean, you're in Japan where the concept that you're never truly a master exists,

and you're always learning the craft. You may be called a "master copywriter" but you're really a student, because in terms of what there is to know and what's always changing, it doesn't end.

CML: Perhaps many people have come to think of you as a fairly hard-headed, "nuts-n-bolts" type of businessman. But you just recently released your newest book. You mentioned it a little bit earlier.

Joe: Yes, *Spiritual Marketing*. I know where you're going with the question, and it's the other side of what might be perceived as "Mr. Fire" (Mr. Fire is my nickname and handle), and here I come out with this kind of "touchy-feely," whimsical, airy-fairy in some respects, metaphysical book.

CML: A bit of a change of pace.

Joe: Well, it's perceived as a bit of a change because I haven't been out in the open with it, but the reality, the truth (and you and many of your listeners are hearing this for the first time) is that *Spiritual Marketing* (my inside-out approach to marketing) has been how I've led my business and my life for decades.

I've only recently come out of the closet about it and made it public by writing a book on it, but even that book was not fully intended for publication. When I wrote it, it was a little pamphlet that I wrote for my sister. She was on welfare, she was basically having health problems, financial problems, she was struggling in her life, and I thought, "Oh God, there are some things, if she only knew them, that would make a difference." And I wrote this little pamphlet called *Spiritual Marketing* for her.

As it evolved, I gave it to a speaker one time as a gift, and he announced that book in front of 250 people at his seminar...

CML: And you weren't ready.

Joe: And I wasn't ready, no. Sixty people – literally sixty people – came up wanting that book right then and there. I realized that there's a market for this. People are ready for this. I don't have to hide my spiritual side. So in some ways, it's a shock for people to hear that Joe "Mr. Fire" Vitale has come out with Spiritual Marketing, but in other ways, it's just the real me.

CML: Where can listeners find the book?

Joe: Amazon sells it, so that's a good way to get it. It's also listed on my website, http://www.mrfire.com, and http://www.1stbooks.com is the publisher of the book. But I always drive people to Amazon. It's one of my favorite places to shop, so go to Amazon and get it.

CML: Including your eBooks, how many books does this make now, Joe?

Joe: I don't know. I think it's eleven – well, it could be thirteen. I do have a couple of books that aren't published yet, and I will be publishing them, so it's in the neighborhood of a dozen.

CML: That's a good stack of books.

Joe: Yeah, it is. It's my own little library.

CML: You talk about your "Five Step Formula" in the book. Can you explain this a little bit?

Joe: Wow, The Five Steps in *Spiritual Marketing*. The first is to know what you don't want. Most people are real hung up on what they don't want. They're always complaining, they're gossiping, they're saying they're hurting, they don't have money, they don't have the health that they want. They're stuck on this stage.

And I'm saying, Step One is know what you don't want, because you use it as a springboard to Step Two, which is know what you DO want. That's a very powerful single step.

I have learned about the power of intention. Intention can reshape the universe to your will. And it comes from making a decision for what you want, which is Step Two in *Spiritual Marketing*.

Step Three is to get clear, meaning that if there are beliefs within you saying that "I don't deserve the things that I want," or "it's not possible to get the things that I want," or "there are other things that may have to happen before I can have what I want," those are all beliefs. Get those beliefs out of the way so you're streamlined to go for what you want. And Step Three is all about that; that's getting clear.

Step Four is feeling right now what it would be like to have, do or be the thing that you want. So if it is to drive the new car or live in the new house or have this particular romance, this relationship, feel it. Feel it as if it's happening right this minute because the more you can feel it right now, the more you turn yourself into a magnet for the thing you want. And it will start to come to you as you start to go to it. That's Step Four, feel it.

Step Five is let go. Step Five is let go, because so many of us are still trying to struggle with life and make things happen, and I've actually found the escalator through life.

And the escalator through life is these five steps that I put under the title of *Spiritual Marketing*.

CML: I like that phrase, "escalator through life."

Joe: Well, we've all struggled. I mean, I've been there. I starved in Dallas twenty years ago. I was homeless, I shoplifted to eat. I tell this story in *Spiritual Marketing*. And we've all gone through some of that.

My sister was the same way. Now, the real miracle about this is that I gave her a copy of the new edition of Spiritual Marketing, the one that's in hard cover and in paperback now, and she wrote me a letter. Now this is the same woman who was on welfare, struggling, didn't know where her money was going to come from, trying to raise three kids. She read my book and wrote me a letter saying, "Joe, I read Spiritual Marketing. Great book. I went out and bought a new car right afterwards."

I thought she was kidding. I thought she was being skeptical and being humorous and kind of digging at me saying, "Yeah, a whole book about miracles, right. I went and bought a new car." She did. I talked to her, and she literally did.

So what I'm saying is, yeah, we all know where the rocky road of life is. Most of us are still on it. Most of the people that are driving to work and crying as they're at work, or they're in pain, they're in agony of some sort and don't know that there's an escalator.

I've found it!

CML: I have one question.

Joe: Only one? Okay.

CML: Only one – about this Five Step Formula, the one that was hardest for me was Step Three. Getting clear of all the negative and limiting beliefs. That's still a battle sometimes. Any suggestions or hints there?

Joe: Yeah, that's a good point. That <u>is</u> a toughie. See, most of us don't get anywhere – or don't move very fast or very much forward in our lives because we're still within our own box. We're in our own frame of reference. The story I talk about in Spiritual Marketing to illustrate this, is that I had a dog in college that I never put on a leash and I always let it run. Of course, it tore up the garbage and tore up the gardens and ran out in traffic and just generally raised hell and was a total nuisance to all my neighbors.

So I put the dog on a leash, and I felt terrible about putting her on a leash. It was a little three-foot leash, and I thought, "That's plenty for her." But she'd run and try to play and was totally restricted.

Then, weeks later I went and got a six-foot leash. I put the six-foot one on her, and I said, "Come on, come on." But she only went three feet. She went the length of what she had been trained was her boundary.

I had to go, put my arm around her and walk her the other three feet and say, "Look, you've got a lot more room here."

CML: Joe, this sounds like a lot of people's lives, a lot of people's childhoods.

Joe: This is exactly the point. It is, and the metaphor goes on because I was a coach to her. I think we all need some kind of "miracles coach" to show us we don't have the boundaries we think we have.

CML: Right.

Joe: That's the answer to getting clear. That whole chapter is pretty long in *Spiritual Marketing,* because I talk about doing a lot of work with a mentor, that I went to for ten years. And I still go to mentors like that. I think we all need to have a coach, a mentor, a counselor, a mastermind group, something that contains a person or persons who are already successful where we want to be successful. They can show us our limitations, our leash, our boundaries, our beliefs, and we can go, "Oh, I didn't realize I can have more, be more or do more." So that's the key to me – it's seeking help.

CML: We'll get back to that in a little bit. I want to cover this in a little more depth, but first, with this same Five Step Formula, just before that, on page 81, there is a phrase that I love, Joe. It goes something like this: "The hardest part to creating life the way you want it, is learning to stop figuring out how you will get what you want." Can you tell us what that means to you?

Joe: That's really with Step Five in letting go, because most of us are still trying to mold life and direct life and orchestrate life. And I swear, Charles, I have had some incredible miracles in my life, and these were things I could not personally orchestrate.

For example, when I was writing one of my most popular books, *The Seven Lost Secrets of Success* (and I tell this story in *Spiritual Marketing*, so you might remember it), I was called out of town to work with a doctor who wanted me to write his book. He wanted to have a book written, and he didn't want to write it, so he wanted to hire me.

I was very reluctant. I was working on The Seven Lost Secrets of Success. I had my own agenda, but something inside of me said, "Oh, go on out there; you're going to get paid and you can use the money; it'll help carry you through while you're writing your own book." So I went, I met with him, I signed an agreement, and he gave me a non-refundable check for several thousand dollars.

Then I came back to Houston where I was living at the time, and I started working on my own book, just kept going. After a month or two, I thought, "Oh, I should be working on the doctor's book." So I called up there to the clinic and nobody answered the phone. At the doctor's clinic, nobody was there to pick up the phone. It's sounding ridiculous, but I called during normal hours and nobody was there.

CML: This is sounding like *Twilight Zone*. The guy didn't exist?

Joe: Well, in a way, he didn't, because three days later, when I finally did get hold of somebody, I spoke to his business manager, and he was very sheepish. I told him who I was, and he said, "Oh, Joe, there've been some changes."

I said, "Like what?"

He said, "Well, the doc's in jail."

And I said, "The doc's in jail?" I mean, this blew my mind. Why was he in jail?

The business manager said, "Well, he violated his parole."

I thought, "What? He was in jail before?" I didn't know any of this.

The behind-the-scenes story was that he had gone through a divorce, he wasn't happy about it, and he started sending bombs to his ex-wife. They put him in prison the first time, and after he served some time, they let him come back out. They let him be a doctor again. He just wasn't allowed to send bombs to anybody anymore. And they found him with bombs in his desk. So they shut him down and put him back in prison.

Now, the punchline is, he had given me a non-refundable deposit to write his book, a deposit that I was able to keep so I could continue writing my own book. And that helped me give birth to *The Seven Lost Secrets of Success*, one of my most successful books, a book that one person so liked that they bought 19,500 copies of it.

How could I have ever orchestrated that kind of funding? I joke in my book, where I say I could have placed an ad that said, "Wanted: doctor who wants me to write a book, give me a lot of money, and then go to jail so I don't have to write his book." I never would have found whom I was looking for. But the universe directed it to me because I had this intention that I wanted to finish *The Seven Lost Secrets of Success*, an important book to me, and I needed the funding to do it.

So the universe, in its wisdom, seeing way beyond my ego's vision, orchestrated all of this.

The same thing happened – can I tell this other story?

Charles: Yeah, sure, please do!

Joe: The same thing happened with my Nightingale-Conant tape set, *The Power of Outrageous Marketing*. I wanted to be in Nightingale-Conant for over ten years. I would send them copies of my books and urge them to consider my work, and say, "I really believe that something like, for

example, *The Seven Lost Secrets of Success*" could be a very powerful, good-selling tape program with Nightingale-Conant." But nothing ever worked. Ten years!

Finally, I just gave up. I thought well, it'll work out or it won't work out, but I'm not going to force it. I'm not going to struggle with it. In other words, I got off of the rocky road and got on the escalator.

One day (I live by my e-mail), I got this e-mail that was from an unknown person who had some questions about P.T. Barnum. One of my books is on P.T. Barnum, the one called, *There's a Customer Born Every Minute*. I answered his questions and didn't think anything of it.

The next day, he asked me another question and I answered it.

The third day, he asked me another question and I answered it.

Then finally, I get this e-mail from him that says, "I'm very grateful for all the time you've taken with me in answering my questions about P.T. Barnum." He said, "If you ever want your material considered by Nightingale-Conant, I'm their senior marketing manager."

I still remember that moment. I had been going up the rocky road and pounding on the front door to get into Nightingale-Conant, and nobody was answering or listening. Then, the universe, God, spirit (whatever you want to call the bigger energy source than what is generated from our own ego) orchestrated it so that somebody, who I don't know, writes to me and I'm kind enough to write back, and it ultimately leads to me having a program with Nightingale-Conant that has become a best-seller for them.

That's letting go.

CML: Wow. Do you have any kind of working definition for luck, or fortune or success that you generally use in your daily life?

Joe: Yeah, I do, and it's not mine. The exact quote is in Spiritual Marketing. It's by Raymond Charles Barker from a book he wrote. I may be paraphrasing it, but I might also have it almost exact: "Success is being able to do what you want to do, when you want to do it."

I love that. Because for the longest time I wasn't able to do that.

CML: Can you say that again?

Joe: Success is being able to do what you want to do, when you want to do it.

The exact quote is in *Spiritual Marketing*; if I can grab a copy, I'll flip through and find it for you.

CML: That's so simple. That's great.

Joe: Well, it's simple, and at the same time, for most of us, it seems like the impossible dream. It is a goal, it is an intention, and it is possible.

That's the beauty of it. It is possible. That's why I used it in *Spiritual Marketing*. I have these little quotations throughout the book that are just inspiring, they're thought-provoking. They're to get people thinking, "Wow, I wonder what else is possible?"

I believe anything is possible and everything is possible.

Here it is. It's by Raymond Charles Barker, 1954, in a book he wrote, *Treat Yourself to Life*: "Prosperity is the ability to

do what you want to do at the instant you want to do it." That's his quote.

CML: I like that. Yeah.

I think our listeners will like that, too, but you know, most people don't live that way.

Joe: No.

CML: You tell a little bit in your book how your life wasn't always like it is now. You went through a fairly long "bad luck" spell. Did you ever feel like life or the universe was a "reverse mechanism" where for everything you wanted to do, it would trick you around the other way?

Joe: Yes. Yes, absolutely. You know, I tell stories. I think I've already mentioned that I starved in Dallas and shoplifted to eat. In Houston I struggled for over a dozen years and lived in a very poverty-stricken area, struggling to do my work, and feeling like nothing I was doing was working out.

I remember when I first got to Houston in the late seventies, early eighties, and I took jobs as a laborer, as a taxi driver, as a reporter, a car sales person. And I remember being phenomenally unhappy.

CML: I can identify with this.

Joe: I can remember being so unhappy that, you get to the moments where you think, "Why live?" If this is life, why do you want to keep living it?

Part of what kept me going was curiosity, because I kept thinking, "What's next? What will happen next? What will shift next?" I think that I always had some sort of vein of optimism in me, though at times, I think back on some terrible moments when that optimism wasn't there at all. It was as bleak and as black and as dark and as pessimistic as anybody could imagine.

Yes, I've been there. And I think it's not unusual; I think we all have. It's just a matter, for many of us, we're are still stuck there. And they don't have to be. I think in *Spiritual Marketing* I have this one section, which I think is titled "It Can Be Another Way." That's part of my message in the book; it's part of the message I wanted my sister to have; it's part of the message other people have given me; it's part of the message I'd love for others to hear – that it can be another way. However it is for you right now, if you really don't like it, it can be another way.

CML: When you think about your life now, Joe, do you feel like you've come out the other side?

Joe: Oh, absolutely. Oh, I live a miraculous life. Right now, as I'm sitting here, I'm in this beautiful home, on the second floor looking out over oak trees and acreage that I now own. I've got a beautiful car that I've always wanted. I've got this beautiful girlfriend. I've got new books coming out that are doing phenomenally well. I've got the income that I've wanted. And it's passive income. That was one of my goals. I didn't want just income; I wanted it to come if I was sleeping or eating or traveling or whatever.

I live a miraculous life. Every time I turn around, there's something majestic taking place. Most of the time it comes as an absolute surprise to me because I just allow it to be there.

I'm always setting intentions; I think that's part of directing fate or increasing your luck, by stating what you want.

You know, it's part of the Spiritual Marketing formula. And I'm also letting go. It's basically pointing and saying, "You know, I want to go over there," and then taking the escalator and letting it take me there.

CML: Do you feel like there was like one major factor or one deciding moment when you learned to make your life more predictable?

Joe: I would say that the one single thing that has made the most dramatic transforming difference in my life has been my work with Douglas Norment, the counselor, the mentor I talked about heavily in the chapter on getting clear in *Spiritual Marketing*.

He was to me like I was to my dog, in the sense that I showed my dog that he had more freedom. Douglas has shown me that I have more power, more freedom, more influence, more energy, more impact than I ever came close to imagining in my life. And I'm a guy who came from a background – I had been a New Age journalist for years. I had interviewed gurus and healers and authors and speakers who talked about magic and miracles in your life.

CML: So you knew about all of this stuff.

Joe: I knew <u>of</u> it from an intellectual level. I did not experience it. That's the key difference. I had dealt with Barry and Suzie Kaufman who had healed their children and many others of autism. They have an institute in Massachusetts called *A Place for Miracles*. And I studied with them. I know them.

I've interviewed authors who are very famous, who talk about creating miracles in your life by learning how to control your own energy.

I knew all of this. I met these people. I had breakfast with many of them. I wrote about them. I reviewed their books.

I wasn't living it.

CML: You were like the kid with his nose pressed to the toy store window.

Joe: Oh, yeah. Now I play with those toys, and I own many of them.

CML: Wonderful.

How big a part does feeling like you <u>deserve</u> to have – how big a part does that play?

Joe: Fantastic. That is probably the single stumbling block for most people, and it was for me, too.

It's the idea that you deserve it, that you can have it, that you're worth it. You know, it's learning to like yourself, and even bigger, it's learning to love yourself.

You know, you and I were in Atlanta (at John Harricharan's SuperSeminar 2001) and we heard a speaker there say one of the hardest questions he ever asked, was to look in the mirror and ask himself, "Do I love me?"

That is powerful. I would say that is the single most powerful thing for someone to get over, to realize, "Okay, miracles are possible; I deserve them, too; I am good enough; I am enough to have them now."

I knew a counselor at one time who used to ask people, "How good can you stand it?" The phrase was implying that you can have more and there could be more. Do you want it? Will you accept it? Do you feel you deserve it? Are you willing to have it? Will you receive it? Will you open your arms? Most people push it away.

CML: Yes, that's the secret, isn't it? Will you accept it?

Joe: Will you accept it, yes.

CML: Because it's there all the time. It's already in existence.

Joe: For example, people that are listening to this right now may be having a variety of thoughts going through their head. But one of the things we can ask is, "We're showing you where the escalator of life is, we're showing you a five-step process (that can even be reduced to one step) on how to create the life that you want and have the things that you want; will you accept it?"

Here it is. Will you accept it? Wow! That's a powerful question.

CML: Being human, we all have our ups and downs, our good days and our bad days. Do you ever find yourself facing a day when you feel like "Oh, I just don't want to motivate myself today," or a period when you feel like "I'm just not really having good luck"? Do you have a set of techniques for putting yourself back on track?

Joe: Well, those don't happen very often any more, but they do still happen. I've met people who say they don't happen at all, and I look at them and think, "Really?"

But it may be the case, and maybe that's where I have to look at it in the sense of, "Well, my life could still be another way." Maybe it is possible to be happy in every single moment, every day. I have to entertain that possibility.

Right now, yes, occasionally I do have those moments where there's a slump or I feel like I'm stuck in negativity. And there is a variety of things that I do – everything from something as simple as taking a nap, because I can just get the energy I need, realign myself to feel better by getting the energy, just getting a little bit of sleep. I may talk it over with somebody. I may meditate. I may do my own Five Step Process and set a new intention for how I want to feel and how I would like to experience things. There's a variety of methods that I've used, everything from the focusing method, to the option method, to Sedona's method. There's a whole bag of tricks.

CML: In other words, you do something. You do something about it.

Joe: Yes, I do something about it. I remember hearing Wayne Dyer twenty years ago say, that if you're really depressed, go get a basketball and shoot hoops. And he followed it up by saying the only thing is take some physical action.

CML: Yeah, change something.

Joe: Change something. Go make a movement, do something. Shift where you're at.

CML: When you face a big new project – to most people, writing a book, especially a non-fiction book with all the research you have to do – that's a big project. Do you ever

have feelings of just being overwhelmed when you first tackle something new?

Joe: Usually, when I first start it, I do. I can think back to the most recent one that required a lot of research was the book I did on P.T. Barnum, *There's a Customer Born Every Minute*.

CML: Great book, by the way. I enjoyed that.

Joe: Thank you very much. I had a lot of fun writing it, discovered a lot about him and about myself. It's a great marketing book and a very entertaining one, and there's even a spiritual quality to that book, too.

I found that when I was hired to write it. The American Management Association, AMACOM, wanted me to write it, I immediately felt overwhelmed. I mean, here was P.T. Barnum who lived eighty very colorful, busy years, and he was far more than a circus promoter. I mean, he was an entrepreneur, he was a publicist, he was a politician, he was a best-selling author, he was a famous speaker. He never said the line, "There's a sucker born every minute," so there was a lot of clearing up of some bad statements that had been made about him.

I thought, "How am I ever going to wrap myself around this man?"

What I had to do was just basically take it one piece at a time, one step at a time. Remember the old thing about how do you eat an elephant? You know, one bite at a time. Even though that's a bizarre thought, the concept is right in the sense that I made an outline and thought, "Well, you know, I'll write whatever's coming up to me first, and

I'll always know that I can rewrite later and edit as I feel; I'll never turn it in until I'm happy with it."

So I just started. I just started and had a blast doing it. One thing led to another; I ended up with a book that I'm very proud of.

You know, A&E on national television, the *Arts & Entertainment* station, did a new biography on P.T. Barnum, and at the end of it, the host said, "Are P.T. Barnum's secrets to success valid today?" And that host, on national TV, held up one book and only one book, which was my book.

And I didn't know he was doing that. Overnight, my book became a best-seller at Amazon.com. The book was completely wiped out of print because there were no copies available after that.

So I went from being overwhelmed, to writing a book that was so noteworthy that it became a best-seller overnight, because a news story loved it.

CML: And all you did was just break it down into bite-size pieces.

Joe: I broke it down. I remember buying a file that had about fifteen folders in it. All those folders were empty, of course, to begin with, and I just started throwing notes in it. I thought, "Okay, Barnum as a politician, I think I'll throw that all in this folder. Barnum as a speaker, I'll throw that in this folder, Barnum as an author in this folder, Barnum as a promoter in this folder. And I ended up just breaking it down into manageable tasks.

As I did my research and came up with more material, it padded the folder. Then when I started writing, I would

just pull out a folder. I'd work on one at a time. I could not write such a very in-depth research oriented book in a week or two. So it was a six-month process of research and a six-month process of writing, to end up with a good book, but doing it one piece at a time.

CML: In virtually everything we've talked about so far, you've mentioned lucky breaks here, lucky breaks there, and they always seem to be something unexpected. Can you tell us a little more about how you set up to attract lucky breaks?

Joe: You know, I like the word "luck" but there's also a feeling that goes with the word that implies you don't have control. And I think we have far more control than what we expect. There's a phrase I heard from Robert Fritz, another author I like. He wrote a book called Creating. I forget the name of his course that he teaches, but his phrase is, "You are the predominant creative force in your life."

I can go even further (and I still struggle with this a little bit), but I have a quote in *Spiritual Marketing*, too, that says, "Everything that happens in your life happens because of the magnet in you." Everything. Now, that one's a tough one to accept because most of us have things that happen to us where we think, "Oh no, I didn't want that, I didn't bring that, I didn't cause that." But I'm really feeling that on some level, yeah, we pulled it to us. On some level, for some lesson, we did.

CML: Maybe, if we'll get around to accepting responsibility for the bad stuff, then maybe we can finally accept more good stuff in our lives.

Joe: I think that's it. I think it is accepting all of it, and then using it to grow.

CML: Speaking of growing, what books or what teachers have helped you to grow?

Joe: Wow, there've been a lot. I mentioned I have a giant library here. I would say, clearly, a book that came out in the fifties by Claude Bristol called *The Magic of Believing,* was a book that changed my life. I read it when I was a kid, fifteen or sixteen years old, reading such a powerful book. That book was about creating your own reality, though I don't think he used those words. He talked about the, "if you believe it you can achieve it," type of mentality. *The Magic of Believing* is so powerful it has gone through dozens of editions, and it's still in print today. So *The Magic of Believing* deeply influenced me.

The works of Barry Neil Kaufman, who I mentioned earlier about healing his son and some other children of autism. He has lots of books out, and those have deeply influenced me.

Boy! There are so many. I've got a lot value from the works of Jerry and Esther Hicks, who channel a spiritual being, or teacher, or mentor, however you want to view that, called Abraham.

And I've worked with a lot of belief therapists. There's one named Mandy Evans who has a book called *Traveling Free,* about dissolving the beliefs in the past that are holding you in old patterns.

There's an old out-of-print book called *The Book of EST*. *The Book of EST* was based on the famous Werner Erhard training that was controversial in the sixties and seventies. Well,

The Book of EST kind of brings that seminar to life, and I remember it impacting me in a way few books had.

Off the top of my head, those are some of the books that got to me.

CML: So there were a lot of steps along the way.

Joe: Oh definitely. A lot of steps along the way.

CML: Have there also been certain people who personally in your life, either knowingly or unknowingly served as mentors to you?

Joe: Yes. I don't know if you mean people I've actually met . . .

CML: Yes.

Joe: Well, Douglas, for example, is one of them. Douglas Norment is the counselor I worked with. He's no longer available, so I haven't been able to use him as a resource. Mandy Evans, whom I mentioned wrote the book Traveling Free, is a beliefs counselor who has been a wonderful friend, a wonderful mentor, a wonderful counselor, a wonderful freeing agent for me personally.

I've probably learned from everybody I've ever met. I hope I have, anyway.

CML: Could you tell us a little bit about your experiences with some of these people?

Joe: Wow. I've got to think about it for a second. I guess I can mention one of the ones with Douglas.

One of the very first ones I ever did with him, and I didn't really know what kind of work he did. He said it was energy work and he could help change the things that were going on in me, so that I could have new experiences happen in my life. And when I went to see him the first time, I was struggling. I mean I was with a wreck of a car. I never knew if it was going to make it someplace or it was going to have to be pushed.

CML: I've been there. Yeah.

Joe: Yeah, we've gone through that, too, and right now I can remember the first time I went to him. I was driving that clunker and it started to stall as I was driving. I remember saying out loud to the car, "Look, you can stop if you want to. I'm going to walk to Douglas or I'm going to hitch a ride to Douglas, or you're going to get me to Douglas, but I'm going there."

Well, it got me there. And through my work with Douglas, which was a lot of work about cleansing and clearing the negative beliefs – I wanted to get a new car, for example, at that time, and I thought it was impossible. My credit was bad, I didn't really have an income, I was self-employed and struggling, and I thought there's no way. So he helped me explore that. We explored everything from "do I want it?" (yes), "do I think I deserve it?" (well, I wasn't so sure so we worked on that).

Then we worked on things like what does it mean if I have a new car? Well, one thing that came up was "what's my father going to say?" How would he feel? Well, he was 2,000 miles away and I hadn't seen him in years, but he was still in my head as a voice, as a belief.

CML: Uh huh, I think everybody has a father and a mother in their head.

Joe: That's right. And most of us – you know, the parents have done wonderful things by getting us to where we're at, but we also have to get to the point where we get beyond their limitations.

I am now at that place, but I had to go through some help with Douglas, for example, to remove those limiting beliefs, to realize my father has his own limiting beliefs, and do I want to keep them or not. Well, I didn't.

Not only did I end up buying a new car, and a year or so later another new car, and another year or so later another new car, another year or so later another new car – at this point I'm driving the car of my most glorious dreams. I'm driving a BMW Z3, which is a 2.8 hotrod, that I've never had so much fun driving in my entire life.

Well, this is the same guy who was driving a clunker and my big concern at the time was, will it make it home? And I thought it was impossible.

CML: And you never would have conceived of this back then.

Joe: I would have thought it was preposterous. I would have thought it was insane.

Well, now I'm at the point where I think, "Oh no, why don't I go wash it?" It's cool, because I'm having fun with it.

You know, to answer your question, it's kind of hard to describe some of the experiences with different counselors and teachers. With Douglas it's very metaphysical and it's very energy oriented. But for me, we're in a belief-driven universe, and as we change our personal beliefs, we can have more of the things we want and we can be far, far happier.

CML: Looking at it from the other side of the relationship, why do you think somebody would decide to mentor other people? What's in it for them?

Joe: Oh, good question. Years ago, I took a seminar with Donna Fisher and Sandy Vilas and it was on networking. It was on people helping other people to get mutual results. They asked this question that was similar to what you asked: "Why would anybody want to help?"

I think it was Donna who said, "How do you feel when somebody asks you for help?" Well, you usually feel good. You usually want to help. There's usually a sense of – I don't know – a natural giving. So I think on one level it feels good for these people to help other people. And I think on another level they're giving back what they have gotten.

CML: They're completing a circuit.

Joe: They're completing a circuit – right, they're completing the circle.

CML: Good answer.

The way you live today, do you feel like you're living a totally free-form life, or is your life fairly carefully planned out now?

Joe: That's a very interesting question. I would say I have intentions. I have long-term and short-term intentions, but I remain open to change. So in other words, it's a little bit like what I mentioned earlier, I'll point in a certain direction and say "I want to go over there." And then I'm going to ride the escalator to get me to it, or to get me to something better than it.

So that requires me to have a sense of where I would like to go, while also having a sense of, "You know, if I get nudged to go over here, it's okay." Because over here might be far better than what I thought was over there.

I'm talking in somewhat general terms because I'm not sure how to answer it more specifically. I am not a person who carefully plans out my day, my life or any of that. I do have intentions.

I learned from Abraham about segment intending, which means you can break up your day into segments, and throughout those segments you can have intentions for each one. For example, oh, forty-five minutes ago, before we started this phone conversation, I had the intention that I was going to give an inspiring, informative, articulate, up-beat conversation with you. You and I would have a great time doing this, and that the people who listen to it down the road will learn something that will make a massive difference in their lives – they'll get more of what they want, they'll be happier in each moment, something will shift for them in a wonderful way.

I set that as an intention. But I didn't go and map out, "Well, I've got to make sure I say this, I've got to make sure I answer a question in this particular way, and there's really this quote – I've got to make sure I say this quote." I didn't do any of that. Out of my intention for where I want to go, a lot of these other things will just bubble up.

You've asked me some questions that have led to things I didn't know I was going to say, but they came out, and you've even acknowledged once or twice like, "Good answer," and I thought, "Well, I didn't know it was a good answer. I didn't even know I was going to say it."

So I'm having an intention, but I also have that fifth step about letting go to something better.

CML: If this were music, it would be like your intention is the theme, and your performance is the jazz that results. Something like that?

Joe: That's a way of describing it, yes.

CML: Do you believe every single person – every person – can improve their life and their luck?

Joe: Absolutely.

CML: No exceptions?

Joe: No, no, no. No exceptions. No. I can't imagine any exceptions.

I know that there will be many people who will refuse the possibility, but I think it goes back to if they accept it, if they accept what's being offered, if they believe it, if they feel they're worth it. You know, all of that internal stuff can be changed. Those are all thoughts.

Those are all thoughts; you can change your thoughts. I know I've also been at the place where I thought, "You can't change your thoughts, not that easily, nah, uh uh."

Well, that's a thought. That very belief, that you can't change your thoughts or it's not easy, is a belief. You can change that, and then you're back to, "Well, I guess I can be happy, I can experience the life that I want, I can have miracles." Yes, every person can improve their life and their luck.

CML: We talked a little while ago about feeling like you deserve good things. What's the very best way for a person to help themselves feel like they deserve good luck or success or good things in life? Let's touch on this again.

Joe: That's a good question. I would say possibly sitting down and remembering some of the good things you've done for yourself or somebody else. Possibly remembering some of your achievements, your accomplishments, and those don't have to be a New York Times best-seller if you wrote a book, or you won a Nobel Prize. They may happen to be something like you helped a neighbor in an emergency, or you made a phone call to your mother and it made a difference. Those kind of things for one.

And then, I would say do something for yourself. In other words, take the bubble bath, or go to the movie that you always wanted to see, or buy yourself that nice dinner, or whatever it happens to be.

CML: It doesn't have to be big and earthshaking.

Joe: No, not at all. It's these little tiny things that send a signal to yourself, almost unconsciously, that say, "I'm okay, I'm worth it, I love myself." It can be the most small, tiniest experience that you and I would think is insignificant, but in some way is important to the person doing it.

CML: Anything to break the momentum in the wrong direction and start the momentum in the right direction, anything, no matter how small. This is what you're saying, right?

Joe: Yeah, it's the baby steps that just lead to bigger steps.

CML: For a person who's up to his neck in problems, what do you suggest they do first? And why?

Joe: If a person is up to their neck in problems, I think they should seek a mentor. I think they should seek somebody who's already successful at what they want to be successful at.

CML: Won't that mentor laugh at them, though?

Joe: No. No, that's the wrong mentor, if they do. I suppose that's an outside chance, but I think when you start to look for the people that will help, like in the back of my Spiritual Marketing I list six or seven different counselors who are available.

You know, Napoleon Hill talked about the power of having a mastermind group. I heard a story the other day. I think it was about Tony Robbins, the famous speaker. Somebody was complaining that they have a mastermind group and they're only making $5 million a year.

CML: Oh, poor guy.

Joe: Yeah, poor guy. He's making $5 million and he wants to make more, but he feels like he's got that leash. He's opened his leash, but he's only opened it to $5 million a year. So he's not going as far as he can see; he's only going as far as he feels he can walk.

So Tony Robbins says, "Do you have a mastermind group?"

And the man said, "Yes, I'm in a mastermind group. We meet weekly and we have various people in there, and we all try to mentor each other."

Tony Robbins said, "How much is the most wealthy person in there making?"

He said, "$5 million a year."

Well, Tony said, "That's the problem, then." He told the man, "I'm in a mastermind group, and I make hundreds of millions of dollars a year, and the most successful person in my mastermind group makes $500 million a year. You need to have another mentor."

So I think we need to have a mentor who's already successful at what you want to be successful at. You began this conversation by asking me about copywriting. One of the mentors who helped me the most when I was struggling and trying to learn the craft was Bob Bly. Bob Bly has written thirty-five books. He has been a prolific advertising genius. He has always answered my questions, he wrote books, he sent me books, he sold me materials, he was always there for me. I met him only once a couple of years ago, and I felt like a little kid who met his superhero.

I told him that. I wrote him a note and said, I felt like a little kid meeting my superhero for the first time. That's how it felt. He gave without wanting anything in return, but that was a mentor, already successful in the field I wanted to be successful at.

CML: He's a great inspiration.

Joe: And he has been to me, and he still is.

I send out a monthly newsletter. People can go to http://www.mrfire.com, my website and sign up for it, but I sent out the most recent one, and Bob Bly wrote me a note and said, "This was the best newsletter you've ever written. How in the world did you ever do it?"

I wrote back and said, "All I do is follow what you do." He's inspiring to me.

So to answer your question about being neck-deep in problems, I think that getting somebody who's already out of it, to help you, is important.

And there are coaches out there. That's another word for a mentor or a counselor. There's nothing wrong with having a coach. You and I met one of the coaches in Atlanta when we were there.

CML: Yeah, Don McAvinchey.

Joe: That's right. He's available. Help is available, and maybe this is another part of it; being willing to ask for help. Being willing to raise your hand and say, "You know, I can't do it on my own, will somebody help?"

CML: And if you've asked for help and somebody laughs at you, as you said, you've asked the wrong person. Move up, move up.

Joe: Yeah, move up is right.

CML: What was the hardest thing in your life to change? And why?

Joe: Probably coming to the place where I felt like I deserve the things I wanted. Probably learning to love myself, learning to like myself, learning to accept myself, learning to be okay with who I am and where I am, while knowing I'm changing and going for who I would like to be. A sense of deserving, a sense of "it's okay to have the things I want in my life." It's not going to hurt other people, it's not going to take away from other people, it's okay if it's more than what my parents had. A sense of deserving was probably the hardest

thing, and once I'd taken care of that, more and more miracles in a magical universe became mine.

CML: Do you feel like you've finally arrived at something like a coasting phase? Or are you still on an uphill track, and you're still learning lots of new stuff?

Joe: Well, I'm still learning, but I'm not on the uphill track. I'm coasting. I'm on that escalator. I've found the escalator, I know where it's at, I get on it every day, and I coast.

CML: How to go uphill without climbing.

Joe: That's the phrase. I'm going uphill without climbing. Yeah, I'm not falling down on rocks and getting all cut up. I'm going uphill.

CML: Does learning get any easier for you, the farther you go?

Joe: Yes, it does get easier. And there's a saying. This is really stimulating, and you may have to chew on it for a little bit, but I have it in my Spiritual Marketing book. It's something Douglas used to say. That is, "If you get the lessons, you don't need the experiences."

If you get the lessons, you don't need the experiences.

So many of us are suffering, and we will suffer until we get the lesson of that suffering. If we got the lesson of it before the suffering, we would never have the suffering.

CML: This is important.

Joe: This is very major. This is breakthrough information. I mean, it's going to be a little tough for a lot of people who hear it for the first time, and even after that, to understand it and accept it. But I love it. I've reminded myself of that. You know, if there were any of those bumps in the road or the old dark times, or a day where I feel like I'm in a slump, I may have to look at it and say, "Okay, what's the lesson? What am I trying to tell myself? What do I need to learn here?" Because the quicker I learn it and I get it, the quicker I'm out of it.

If you get the lessons, you don't need the experience.

CML: I know that for most people, learning new things can be pretty stressful. Do you think we ever reach a point where we can just relax and enjoy every – every – new learning experience?

Joe: I think that's the definition of enlightenment. I think that's enjoying each moment. That's being aware of each moment. That's appreciating each moment. That's living in each moment. That's seizing each moment. I absolutely do believe we can relax and enjoy it and learn in each moment. It probably comes from one of the greatest challenges of all time, <u>being here now</u>.

Most of us are thinking back to the last question you asked, for my answer, or moving forward to "what's he going to ask next?" but not right here where my breath is. Where I am. Where you are. You're in Japan. I'm out in the hill country of Texas. In this moment is a shared, magical miraculous, wonderful experience that we can relax and enjoy as we're learning.

CML: You just said something which, the implications of that just kind of blow me away. You didn't say it directly, but I'm going to rephrase this.

Joe: Yeah, tell me. I'm interested.

CML: The enlightened person doesn't know everything, but the enlightened person can relax and enjoy learning new stuff.

Joe: Oh, you're right. That's a massive statement. There is no "knowing everything." That's an impossibility, in my mind. There is no knowing everything.

We talked about copywriting. I'm supposed to be a hotshot copywriter. I don't know everything about copywriting. I supposedly know about metaphysics and I wrote about spiritual marketing. I don't know everything about that. I never will. I wrote one of the most well respected books on P.T. Barnum. I'm considered a P.T. Barnum expert. I'm not P.T. Barnum; I don't know everything about his life. There are entire holes I'll never know anything about.

My goodness, it's an ego trip to think we are going to know everything. We have to let that go so that we can enjoy everything that we can know in this moment.

CML: Do you have any advice for people who don't really like to learn new stuff?

Joe: Yeah, be happy.

CML: Be happy.

Joe: Be happy.

I learned from Barry Neil Kaufman in his research (and it's all about being happy now), most of his research is saying that the miracles come from being happy. He said that happy people (and this is the one step: I mentioned earlier that *Spiritual Marketing* has five steps to it and I can reduce it all to one step, this is so profound), the idea that Barry's research showed that happy people tend to go for and get their goals more often than unhappy people.

Unhappy people tend to use unhappiness as a type of motivator. They get angry enough, they'll take action. They get unhappy enough, they'll take action. What he found is that they just get unhappy, they don't take any action. Or if they do take any action, they don't achieve anything. They're going up the rocky road; they're not going up the escalator.

CML: They're just dodging rocks.

Joe: They're dodging rocks, dodging bullets (perceived bullets), but they're not achieving what they want. Happy people tend to get more of what they want, and even when they don't, they're still happy.

CML: Just one or two more things. Let's turn to the future now, totally different subject.

Many teachers say the earth experience is about to change really significantly. How do you envision our daily life changing in the next fifty or one hundred years, or the next five hundred years or so? This is far out stuff.

Joe: It is far out because I have no idea. I don't know.

I'm going to say first that human nature is never going to change, and that's wonderful that it won't. People are still going to be moved by their passions. They're still going to want love and money and romance and health and happiness. All of those key, core emotions, those drives are never, ever going to change. They've never changed since the beginning of time; they're never going to change.

The things that will change will be the technology and our life style, our way of living. And I believe it's going to become more fascinating, more interesting, more exciting than ever before. If somebody had said seven or eight or nine years ago that there would be an Internet, I didn't know it was coming. That was only, what, within the last ten years? How am I going to predict fifty to a hundred years? Or five hundred? Something so fantastic is going to take place that the most brilliant science fiction writer can't even paint it because he can't even imagine it.
I'd say hold on for a wonderful ride.

CML: I like your vision of the future. Do you have any final words of advice to our listeners who may still be floundering around trying to get out of the starting gate?

Joe: Well, sure. My self-serving bit of advice is go get *Spiritual Marketing* at Amazon.com and enjoy that. But the larger, more global, less self-serving advice would be, you know – maybe I can say it this way: people have asked me what I think I owe my successes to. And I said (and this is what I would advise people to do), I follow my enthusiasms.

I follow my enthusiasms. It's very close to the Joseph Campbell phrase of "follow your bliss."

All I've done is, I was excited about P.T. Barnum so I wrote about P.T. Barnum. I was excited about Bruce Barton, an advertising genius who is long gone, and I wrote about him for *The Seven Lost Secrets of Success*.

I've been fascinated with spiritual marketing, so I wrote about that, primarily for my sister. I have followed my enthusiasms. So I would say, follow your bliss. Follow the things that excite you. Follow the things that you get enthusiastic about. Go there.

CML: Great.

For our listeners, you can visit Joe's main website at http://www.mrfire.com, and you can get Joe's new book, *Spiritual Marketing*, at http://www.1stbooks.com and now also at http://www.amazon.com where he gives his very special take on life, luck and success in the new book, *Spiritual Marketing*.

Joe, we've used up all our time. I want to thank you again for speaking with us today.

Joe: Thank you. I've had a marvelous experience.

****

Charles Burke is the author of "Command More Luck," a book offering powerful suggestions on getting more cooperation from life, luck, and your own mind. Stop waiting around for good things to happen. Whether you call it synchronicity, or serendipity, or just plain old luck, you CAN become more "naturally lucky." To find out more, visit the More Luck website at: http://www.moreluck.com

****

Printed in the United States
84993LV00002B/19/A

9 781600 371899